$7.95

BORN TO LOSE

ED MORRIS

All his life people have told Ed Morris he was an animal. For 22 out of 40 years, society had caged him like one. Is it any wonder he had lived always on the edge between breaking the law and going straight?

Born in the explosive South Bronx area of New York, young Morris learned stealing as a way of life. All he knew of family living was the constant abuse and neglect of one foster home after another. The years passed, and it seemed to Morris that whether he took a straight job in a bakery or went on sticking up liquor stores, he landed in jail — beaten, homosexually raped, and thrown in strip-cell isolation for days on end.

On one level, Ed Morris's autobiography is a two-fisted indictment against society's shabby correctional system and the hypocrisy that labels it "rehabilitative." But **BORN TO LOSE** is more than a commentary on the injustices of our penal system; it is a plea for understanding through one man's fight for survival.

BORN
TO LOSE

BY

Ed Morris

 Mason & Lipscomb PUBLISHERS   NEW YORK

"Epistle to Augusta" from the book LETTERS by Lord Byron. Preface by Prof. R. G. Hogarth. Everyman's Library Edition. Published by E. P. Dutton & Co., Inc. and used with their permission.

Library of Congress Cataloging in Publication Data

Morris, Ed, 1932-
   Born to lose.

   1. Morris, Ed, 1932-   I. Title.
HV28.M68A34   365'.6'0924 [B]   74-12021
ISBN 0-88405-090-4

Produced by Whitehall, Hadlyme & Smith, Inc.

This book is dedicated to those special people
who opened their hearts to me
and to
All those still suffering because of an uncaring society
and to
The love-filled younger generation, who refuse to be
blinded by the hypocrisies of their elders

MINE WERE MY FAULTS, AND MINE BE THEIR REWARD.
MY WHOLE LIFE WAS A CONTEST, SINCE THE DAY
THAT GAVE ME BEING, GAVE ME THAT WHICH MARR'D
THE GIFT, A FATE, OR WILL, THAT WALK'D ASTRAY;
AND I AT TIMES HAVE FOUND THE STRUGGLE HARD,
AND THOUGHT OF SHAKING OFF MY BONDS OF CLAY:
BUT NOW I FAIN WOULD FOR TIME SURVIVE,
IF BUT TO SEE WHAT NEXT CAN WELL ARRIVE.

—Lord Byron
from Epistle to Augusta

Prologue

The problem with writing a book is not knowing where to start or where to stop. It is even more difficult when you are writing a life story like mine. So much has happened, so many incidents of anguish and pain have been lived through that one wonders if the reader will find them of any consequence.

I guess I'll start where I first thought of writing a book on my life: in the hospital while recovering from gunshot wounds. But first, I would like the reader to understand clearly that the purpose of this book is not to evoke sympathy or the attitude "poor guy, never had a chance." Its purpose is to awaken the public to the desperate need for the reevaluation of treatment for the neglected child and for the criminal offender.

My story is not unique. Thousands of people have gone through life filled with the torments I suffered, and filled with the same thoughts of loneliness, desperation, confusion and a need for love and acknowledgment.

Let us begin.

1

I opened my eyes, and strained to focus them. My vision was blurred, and my mind dull. Slowly the shape of the IV bottle came into reality and as I looked around, I realized I was alive. It came as a surprise and a sense of disappointment filled my being. I had expected to die, I had wanted to die, yet here I was, still alive. Even in death I was a failure. The pain started hitting me—my chest, my back, my arm. I attempted to roll over into a more comfortable position when a sharp pain reminded me I had also been shot in the head. A nurse came into view, discovered I was awake and soon some doctors came. No sooner did they start asking me how I was feeling than the cops came in. After the doctors finished taking my pulse, etc., they left the room telling the cops, just a few minutes. Who did it? Why? What were you doing in our town? We know you were trying to run dope in our town. So you guys are starting a gang war in our town. Well, we're not going to let it happen even if we have to kill everyone of you bastards. Then the nice guy cop took over. He chased the rest out of the room, and started talking to me, oh so nice: "Listen are you going to let them bastards get away with this? Help us out and we'll take care of you. We know about your robbery case in New York. You got a long record and you need our help."

I told him I didn't know anything and drifted into unconsciousness.

I awoke again hearing a woman's voice. Immediately, I was filled with a sense of warmth and love. Lori was here. We talked softly, not mentioning the reasons for my getting shot. She was scared and I could sense it. I assured her it was all over but she didn't believe me. I told her I was sorry I dragged her into this, but I called for her because I didn't want to die alone, and lonely. I wanted to die with the warmth of her love and the sight of her beauty. And she was responsible for my being alive. Until the cops said she was coming, I was willing myself to die. Then I fought to live only to see her.

The days went by, and I realized I was in a very expensive hospital, and was somewhat a celebrity among the patients and nurses. Not many people survive from five bullet wounds. Plus the papers had made me out as a major gangster trying to corrupt a small town by trying to run dope, gambling and who knows what. What a crock of shit. The night I was shot was the first night I was ever in the town. I quickly realized that I was going to be the scapegoat for all the shit going on in the town. The cops told me they had received a phone call giving them all the information about me and what I was trying to do. This was going to be one hell of a setup. And it certainly wasn't going to help my case in Manhattan. The irony of the whole situation was the fact I had been trying to go straight. What a fucked-up life. Couldn't anything ever work my way? Couldn't I do anything right or ever get any kind of break? I began thinking about my life and it is these thoughts I am now writing about. Was it me that somehow caused all the rotten luck? Or are there some people destined to be one of the lost?

2

The earliest remembrances of my life are unhappy ones, as are most of my memories. I first remember being in children's shelter with a lot of other parentless children, with not enough people to watch us or take care of us. I remember on certain days, prospective foster parents would come in to look at us and decide which of the kids they would take. This was a big occasion for us kids. The chance to be taken out of the foundling hospital and be given parents. We would get all spruced up and clean and try our damnedest to impress the grownups. It was exciting, and something we really looked forward to, yet it was a very unhappy experience for most of us. Each time we'd get our hopes up that this time we would get picked, that somebody would like us, but then they would pick some other kid, and those left would naturally feel so unwanted. It was there that I guess I first began to think I was different from other kids. Something was wrong with me; no one wanted me, and I didn't know why. I mean after all, I knew I had parents; no one had told me they were dead, and instinctively I knew they were alive, and even they didn't want me. Something was wrong with me, but no one would tell me what.

The other big highlight of the hospital was that directly across the street was a place where the firemen would go through their tests and drills, clambering up and down ladders, and jumping into life nets. This was always exciting to watch.

Next I remember living with a German family named Cliffield, I believe. They were very pro-German, and this was at the height of Hitler's killing Jews in Europe. I was constantly called Jewish scum, and cursed at in German. Why they took me as a foster child is beyond me, unless they couldn't get any other child from the social service, because of their being considered poor foster parents. I was probably offered to them only because the foster service couldn't get anyone else to take me. These people were absolutely sick in their attitude towards me. Two of my sisters were there also, but for some reason they weren't treated as badly as I was. I was about six years old then. They had a big farmhouse, and their son delighted in playing tricks on me, and constantly was the cause of my getting punished. We all had to work on the farm, and it seems I was always the one working after everyone else had finished their chores. There was some chore I had to do in which I had to use some kind of shears. The shears would constantly close on the heel of my hand, and the skin became very raw and extremely painful. The son would keep bringing me more and more work, and then when it took me a long time to finish he would say he only brought me a little bit of work. So this would result in more cursing and punishment. I would always have to go right to my room in the evenings, instead of being allowed to play. It seemed I was always in trouble and never knew why. I would lay in my bed and try to figure out what was so different about me compared to other children. Even worse, I didn't understand about Germany and Jews and all that.

Right next to my room there was a bathroom, but I was not allowed to use it, nor were my sisters. We had to use the outhouse, even in the winter, and believe me there was lots of snow and cold. For years afterwards, I associated taking a crap with being cold. If I had to piss during the night, I would sometimes sneak into the bathroom and piss in the sink, and slowly run the water to rinse out the piss. I wouldn't piss in the toilet as it made too much noise when you flushed it. Other times, I would just piss out the window. One morning I awoke and my room smelled of shit. I searched around and found where someone had taken a crap in a corner between the dresser and the window. I got scared to death. I would be given a bad beating for this. Before I had time to think of what to do the son came into my room telling me to hurry down to breakfast. He saw what I was looking at and hollered for his mother. She came up and seeing the shit on the floor, she went berserk hitting me and cursing me and calling me Jewish filth. She beat me to the floor and then grabbed me behind the neck and pushed my face in the shit. She pushed so hard, my face scraped against the floor and was scratched. She rubbed my face all around it until my face was completely covered with the stuff. I gagged and could hardly breathe; I thought I would die. Some of it got in my eyes and it burned, and where it got into the scratches on my face it burned terribly. I was terror stricken. I had to scrub the floor until all trace and smell was gone from the room, before she let me clean the shit off my face. It was horrible, but my fear of her was even worse. Finally I had to go outside and clean with ice cold water. The more I scrubbed my face, the more it hurt, and I made all the scratches on my face worse. At first I thought perhaps one of my sisters had done it, because they may have been afraid to go out, it was so cold out. They swore they didn't do it. Then I thought the son might have done it just to get me in more trouble. I never did find out who did it. This incident is still very real and fresh in my mind, even today.

I was constantly hollered at, and I lived in fear for my life. I hated waking up and dreaded leaving my room in the morning. And at night I would invariably cry myself to sleep, wondering why these things happened. And the fact that I didn't know, that I couldn't find any rhyme or reason why these things happened to me, made it all the worse.

And then came that Christmas Day. We lived two miles from the church and school and I had been told never to hitch a ride. Several times I did and when it was discovered, I was beaten and punished. Well, this Christmas Day I had to stay a bit late, because I helped at the mass. I carried a candle during the service, and there were cookies, etc. for the altar boys. This caused me to miss the bus and it would be a long time before another came. The cop outside the church knew me, as he did most of the kids, and when I explained the situation to him he stopped a car in which he knew the family was going past my house and asked them to drop me off. As soon as I got out of the car and saw them standing on the porch looking at me, I knew I was in for it. Not listening to anything I tried to say, she slapped me around, and the more I hollered the more she beat me. Then she said that a rotten Jewboy like me should not be allowed to play with other children on Christmas Day. I remember my sisters were more interested in playing with their presents, than me getting beat. I was put down in the cellar with the lights off, and the door locked. I was petrified with fear because of the mice and rats. I screamed and hollered for so long that finally I just broke down and couldn't scream any longer. I cried uncontrollably for hours. I stood at the

9

bottom of the stairs, afraid to move and hoping they would open the door and let me come back up. But they didn't. I heard them all sitting down to dinner, and I just knew they would call me up then, but they didn't.

And then came a different kind of feeling. A feeling that was ultimately to become a pattern of my whole life. Of course I didn't recognize it then. I became completely disgusted, I was crying, I was cold, I was terrified, and then I became angry. I just felt I had to do something to change the immediate situation, something drastic, anything to get out of there. Anything had to be better than this. I gave no thought to the consequences of what I was going to do. I have been confronted with many desperate situations during my years, and I dealt with them just as I did that day in the cellar.

My decision then was to burn the house down. I gave no thought to my being hurt. And I certainly didn't care if anyone else got hurt. I spread all the old newspapers in the cellar and the burlap bags all over the floor. Then I took burning coals out of the furnace with a shovel and spread them on the papers and bags. Very quickly the flames shot up. For a while I was fascinated with the sight. Then I calmly broke out a window, and climbed up to the ground. I ran to the edge of the road, oblivious to the snow and the cold. Almost immediately the flames were shooting out of the window I had broken. It seemed strange. I remember comparing the flames to those out of a dragon's mouth. Quickly the bottom of the house was wrapped in flames. Everyone came running out of the house hollering. I hated them all, but when I saw her, I was angry she got out. I wanted her to die; she had no right getting out. I felt terribly disappointed. I really, really remember the feelings I had then. I wanted to somehow push her into the fire. Everyone came running to where I was standing, and I guess they didn't realize what had happened, and how come I was already out there. They were just so glad they got out. When they all got next to me, I stepped apart a little from them and wished somehow I could erase them all. I wanted them out of my life or else I would always suffer. By the time the firemen got there the house was badly burned. I don't think it could have been repaired and I never found out because after staying the night in a neighbor's home, the social worker came and took us away. I am sure they later figured I had something to do with the fire, but no one came right out and said I did it. I think it was because then they would have had to explain why I was punished in such a manner, and a lot more of their treatment towards me would have come out. The firemen questioned everyone and even asked me if I knew what happened. Of course I said no.

I was put in another home without my sisters. We weren't ever put in a home together again. This next home was just a big blank. I don't remember much about it. There are very big gaps in my memory up to the age of ten. In one home, the parents weren't too bad, as far as I can remember. I can't recall too much about them, but I do remember their son. He was older than me, about sixteen, I think. I think at that time I was about eight. He was always playing tricks with me, teasing me and getting me into trouble. One time, the parents were out and he called me into the bathroom. He had his prick out, and at first I guess I thought he was just going to the toilet. He was pulling it and playing with it. I didn't know what he was doing, and I didn't know if it was good or bad, him calling me in there. His prick started getting hard, and I was curious. I never saw anything like this before. But I knew something was wrong then. I got scared and I wanted to leave; something wasn't right. As I turned to leave, he grabbed me with his free hand and pulled me alongside him. He told me to touch it, but I wouldn't. He tried coaxing me but I refused. I just knew it wasn't right to do. I started crying, hollering for him to let me go. He

11

slapped me and told me to shut up or else he would really beat me. I just kept crying, and the tears were pouring down my face. I felt so fucked up inside. I didn't know what he was going to do, but I was scared. He forced my hand on his prick and made me masturbate him. Every time I started pulling my hand away, he squeezed my neck and it hurt real bad. Finally white fluid came out of his prick. He let my hand go. I didn't know what the fuck happened, or why white stuff came out. He told me if I ever told on him, he would kill me, and besides no one would believe me anyway. He swore he would never make me do it again, and at the same time he told me that was the mark of a man, when you could make that white stuff come out of your prick. He told me I didn't know what it was all about, that I was too young to understand, that it wasn't really bad, and that when I got to be a man I'd understand. I went back to my room, and cried myself to sleep. Not too long after though, I began thinking about what he said about being a man and it being a sign of being grown up. So I began trying it. I wanted to be a man, a grownup. And I kept trying it but it never happened with me. I used to get a strange kind of feeling and just when I thought it might happen, it never did. I began thinking I could never be a man, no matter how hard I tried. I started feeling sorry for myself. What was wrong with me that I could never be a man. I was completely torn up inside. I had no one to talk with. Certainly not the nuns in school. All I associated with them was getting slapped.

The next family I lived with was up in the Bronx, on Bainbridge Avenue. I wasn't happy living there, but there wasn't anything extremely bad about it. I guess I equated living conditions with how bad I was treated. My father visited me once in a while. He was living with my mother, but for some reason I couldn't live with them. One time he brought me a watch. It was a cheap watch, but to me it was

12

great. My father did care about me, I thought; he gave me something. I showed all the kids in the street and in school my watch my father gave me. They all knew I was a foster child and teased me about not having a father or mother. Now I had the watch to show them I did have a father. I was somebody. At night, I put it on the table next to my bed, and it was the first thing I reached for in the morning. One morning it was gone. Panic! I searched the room inside and out, even though I knew I put it on the table. I ran downstairs to the breakfast table and hollered and screamed that they took it. One of their kids must have taken it. The father jumped up from the table and grabbed my ear and told me his kids weren't thieves like me, they were good kids. I kept screaming, I became hysterical, and he started slapping me, and called me an ingrate. He gave me a severe beating because I started cursing him, and called them all thieves for stealing the watch my father gave me. It was the only thing I had from my father. He was yelling who would steal such a cheap watch. This infuriated me even more, because to me it was priceless. I never did find out what happened to the watch. But from then on I was treated very coldly by the whole family.

Another incident I remember in that same house was that a woman in her twenties lived in the room across from mine. I don't know if she was a boarder or who she was. I used to peek through her keyhole at night and watch her undress. It fascinated me, and I began to wait for her to come home each night so I could watch her. One time after she had taken all her clothes off, I saw this white thing between her legs. It was a sanitary napkin, but of course I didn't know it then. I was very puzzled about it. One night she pulled open the door and caught me. She grabbed me, pulled me into her room and closed the door. She said she knew I was peeking in on her many nights. I started crying right away, afraid of her reaction. But she didn't holler at me. She brought me over to her bed and sat down and talked to me in a nice way. She asked why I peeked at her and she spoke to me so nice I stopped crying and began feeling good. It was so long since someone talked nice to me. She asked me if I liked her and did her body seem nice to me. I guess I told her yes. She hugged me to her breasts and said if I kissed them I would feel better. I did kiss them, burying my face into the soft comforting cushions. Then she said she wouldn't tell on me if I did something for her. I guess I told her I would do anything for her, she was so nice, and she liked me. Beside, I knew if she told on me I'd really be in trouble. So I agreed to do anything she wanted me to do. She then lay down and pulled my head between her legs, telling me to kiss her there. I was a little afraid but she seemed so warm and smelled so nice I kissed her hairs, without really knowing why she wanted me to. She smelled so strange there, but sweet, and I tried to bury my head in the warmth among the hairs. She told me to kiss her there and use my tongue, and I did so avidly and greedily. I pushed my tongue in the crevice there that I discovered and as I did so, she squirmed and wrapped her thighs about my head. A strange feeling came over me, that not until years later, could I understand. She tensed her body and thrashed all over the bed. I got scared and tried to pull back, but she hollered not to stop. Soon it was over for her and she relaxed but I lay there not wanting to move. She patted the top of my head and said I was a good boy, and that a man couldn't have pleased her more. I thrilled when she said that, and as she suggested it was time for me to go back to my room, I went back and lay awake feeling I was a man. I tried for several nights to get back into her room, but she always put me off. I never knew why.

I lived with a real nice family later. I wish I could have

14

stayed with them. I'm sure my life would have been far different. I had an earache once in the middle of the night, and I was crying. The mother came in and gave me some medicine, then let me sleep in bed with her between her husband and herself. I enjoyed living with them, and even now I have no other memories but peaceful ones with them. I had to leave because they were going to Europe for the summer and wanted to take me, but they were not allowed to, since I was only a foster child, and they couldn't legally adopt me.

I was put with a family in Throgs Neck. My first impressions, which were to last, were that I could never like them, and I got the same feeling from them. I just lived there. There was no feeling at all. And soon I got to hate them. There wasn't anyone to talk to. Sure there were kids around the block, but I couldn't really talk with them. I wanted someone to say they cared for me, loved me, to hold me, but there was no one.

One day, while playing on the roof of a building across the way, I fell through the rotten wood, and broke my wrist, and I believe my leg. I remember being in a wheelchair, for some time, so I guess something was wrong with my leg. I had to crawl home, and I realized I must have been unconscious for a while since it was now real dark out. I hollered with all my might, but no one came. I cried hard and screamed, but no one came. I started crawling and the pain was terrible but eventually I reached the house. The steps were in front of me, and I knew I couldn't get up them. I hollered and cried, but no one came. I was scared now because it was so late, and they were strict about me coming home on time. I got up the stairs and slumped against the kitchen door. They opened it and their first remark was that I was going to get it for being so late. They were yelling and I was screaming with pain and tears and fear, and the next thing I remember is being in the hospital. I remember on visiting days, all the other children got visits and fruit and toys, but no one came to see me. The hospital was a bad experience because all I did was brood and think about me being different. The nurses tried to get me to play and laugh, but I couldn't.

When I got out I was put with another family. It seemed like no one wanted me to stay with them. The first words these people said was that they knew I was a bad boy in the other homes, and didn't appreciate all that people were doing for me, but I better behave with them, or else I would be sorry. It was in this home that I remember deliberately stealing. They had a son and he would take me to the five-and-ten-cent store, and he showed me how easy it was to steal penknives. Soon I had lots of them and would give them to other kids or sell them for nickels and dimes. Once a knife closed on my finger, and cut the tip pretty severely. I bled profusely, and to this day I have a scar along the tip of my index finger, and the nerves are somewhat dead.

For the first time I was allowed to visit my parents. Until then I knew nothing about them, except the terrible things some of the families would say about them. On Sundays I would get on the train and ride it to the lower end of the Bronx, and visit with them. All the rest of my family were living there. My sisters and stepsisters. Even my grandmother. I asked why I couldn't, and was I so terrible and different that no one would ever want me. My mother started crying and my sisters and soon I was crying. While traveling back to my foster parents, I decided to run away that very night and go with my parents. I went into the house and turned on the shower, and snuck out. I had to sneak on the train, and ran all the way from the train stop to my parents' house. They said they were glad I came, but I really shouldn't have. It was my grandmother that said I should stay. When the foster parents came looking for me, I hid under my grandmother's bed. My grandmother was a very unique strong person. She was very imposing. She had long, pure white hair and I loved to brush it. But she was a drinker. Each month, she got a check from her husband's benefits and she and my mother would drink for what seemed forever. When the money ran out she would become her wonderful self again. Not so my mother. She was constantly fighting with my father. He was in the Merchant Marine, and every time he would come home she would get money off him for food and stuff, but she would always come home with whiskey. My father would sit there and watch her drink telling her not to get drunk again, but there was no stopping her. Her and my grandmother would turn against my father and there would be screaming and yelling and us kids would start crying, but we would be ignored. My father has always been a hard worker, but he was too weak. He should have left then and for sure his life would have been a far happier one. We lived in a tenement, with the bathroom in the hall. It was horribly filthy. The rats would come right in the bathroom while you were sitting on the bowl. I was about ten then, and started staying out late. I stole frequently at the A & P, mostly to feed myself. There was seldom a hot meal at home, usually sandwiches and sometimes just soup. Soon I got in the habit of giving my sisters some of my goodies. If not for these thefts, we would have been constantly hungry. My stepsister, Eva, about sixteen, was the one that tried to take care of me. She was really good to me and always took my side when my mother and father started yelling at me. But she wasn't there often at nights as she had lots of boy friends, and I know she wanted to get away from the house too. One night I was awakened by loud screaming and fighting. My mother, father and her. The last thing I heard was my father telling her to get out of the house and never come back. I ran to her and

17

begged her not to go, but she said she had to. My parents were calling her a tramp and whore. I didn't know what these words meant and wouldn't have cared if I did. She was the only one that cared for me, and I was afraid when she left I would have no one again. She left in the middle of the night, with nowhere to go, just sixteen years old. I told my parents I wasn't staying and I would run away. They started fighting among themselves about whose child I was and I was no good. The next time I saw or heard from my sister was 22 years later. Her life has been hell.

I started staying out all night. I was just ten then. I would hitch on a truck and crawl up to the canvas bin over the cabin of the truck. I'd curl up in the canvas and fall asleep. Sometimes I would wake up in another state, with no idea where I was. Invariably I would be turned over to the police and returned to my parents. The police finally brought the matter to children's court. The judge, believing my parents, that it was my environment that caused my behavior, told my parents they better move or else he would have to send me away. So we moved three blocks. The pattern was repeated, the judge would again say for us to move, we moved one block, and then again one more block. By now I was with a gang and we stole steadily—five-and-dime stores, the supermarkets, staying out all night. Whenever I did come home, it seemed my mother was drunk. One night my father came home and my mother had passed out without making supper. My father got so disgusted he asked me to help carry his suitcases to his car. He drove away.

I was getting picked up often now. Finally my mother told the cops she couldn't do a thing with me, I wouldn't go to school, I wouldn't come home at night and I was worrying her to death. So they put me in Children's Shelter, up in the Bronx, truly a Devil's Island for kids. It was run by these big amazons who must have weighed about 200 pounds each, all of them. I can easily see them working in the concentration camps of wartime Germany. They never said a kind word. We were fed a piece of meat, or a frankfurter and potato, with a glass of mixed evaporated milk for lunch. For supper, it was a peanut butter and jelly sandwich. This was the daily menu. What little recreation time we had was spent in a room in the basement sitting on the floor. I was constantly being punished. I would always talk back, and go into tantrums hollering and screaming about them being mean. For punishment I would be put in the room where all those who wet the bed had to sleep, and they would make me sleep on one of the other boy's pissy sheets. Even at eleven years I was considered the biggest troublemaker. I stayed alone most of the time, dreaming of ways to get even with everybody. My most constant fantasy was to build a fire and burn everyone up. I wanted no one left but me, because I was good and they were all bad people. My parents got me out, but soon I was back in again.

Eventually I was sent to Lincoln Hall for malicious mischief. For some reason I became very religious there. I guess I wanted to believe someone was good and loved me, so I decided since everyone there said God was good and full of love, I would become an altar boy. I was very much afraid of sinning and going to hell and all that, but still I'd get into a lot of trouble. I was the smallest boy in the place and naturally some older and bigger boys would bully me. In all fairness I guess most of the Brothers were good and wanted to do right, but all I began to see were the bad ones. There were a couple of alcoholics and two Brothers that were openly homosexuals. Some of the other kids learned I was Jewish, and everyone started calling me Jewboy. This made me cry cause I couldn't understand it. Here I was the main altar boy almost, and yet I was considered different. I didn't want to be different. I fought back, but almost always got beat be-

19

cause of my size. There were several older boys that tried to rape me in the attic. They were trying to get my pants down but I fought with hysterical panic. They had to let me go because of the noise. For weeks afterward they would taunt me and call me a girl.

My nights were long and miserable. I believed things were going to be this way for the rest of my life. I was never going to be happy. No one cared if I lived or died. I never got visits there and I envied all the boys that did. Their parents would bring them all kinds of goodies, and it seemed they only shared it with the others that got goodies from home. I couldn't adjust there, though I tried hard. I couldn't tell any of the Brothers what was bothering me. I guess I didn't know myself. And beside there was no Brother I felt I could really talk to.

I won respect from the other boys because of the crazy things I would do to get in trouble. At least I was noticed. Eventually because I was getting constantly punished, I first won sympathy from them and then they began accepting me. Most of all though, they liked me because I would never tell on them no matter what they tried to do to me. One time I was accused of doing something I didn't do, and although I knew who was guilty, I took the punishment rather than rat on them. For minor infractions, the typical punishment was one of two things and sometimes both: you would have to hold out your hands palms up, and the Brother would crack you across the hands with a leather strap, or a wooden barrel stave, or a rubber strap. Sometimes you had to get 25 shots on each hand. Corporal punishment was the rule. Another punishment was to have to print a proverb from the Bible 500 times or more. This had to be done in one night. This was very difficult because you couldn't stay up past a certain time. We learned to tie two pencils together and in this way we could do twice the work, but they caught on to that rather quickly. Another common punishment was to have to kneel outside the Brother's room, while everyone else was in bed. Kneeling on a hard marble floor for several hours was hell on your knees. Sometimes the Brother would go to sleep forgetting you were out there and you had to kneel until you got up the courage to see if the Brother was asleep.

Lincoln Hall consisted of 11 cottages, each held 24 boys. There were two Brothers assigned to each cottage. Some were quite mean, and I imagine some had to be pretty decent. I soon learned the quickest way to earn recognition was to get in trouble. No longer was I a nonentity. Everyone knew me in the place, and I gloated over this; the punishment was nothing compared to this. I was somebody. Soon the bigger boys let me hang out with them. One thing for Lincoln Hall, there were plenty of sports, and I always tried the hardest to be the best. I never thought of getting hurt, I'd just hurl myself into whatever game we were playing.

I never conformed, and eventually, after staying longer than most, I was released. But things hadn't changed at home. The fights were frequent, so I ran the streets, coming home whenever I felt like it.

3

I left Lincoln Hall with mixed feelings. As much as I didn't like the place, I at least felt I had a place there, whereas at home, back on the streets I had nothing— not even a corner to call my own. I couldn't stand it at home. My mother and grandmother were constantly drunk, and when my father came home from the Merchant Marine he would get very disgusted. There was no warmth in the house. I started running the streets, and quickly got into shoplifting and burglary. I tried to stay out of the house as long as I could.

I had to report to a probation officer and he made me go back to school. Then I played hookey for long periods. When I did go into school I never brought a notebook or pencil. One particular teacher asked me why I didn't bring a book for taking notes. I told him my mother was too poor to buy me one. So the next day this fuck buys me one and says now I have no excuse. When I showed up in school next time empty-handed, I told him some guys robbed the looseleaf he bought me. I thought it was all a big joke until he tells me to stay after class. After school ended and I saw him in the class, he brings out this big steel ruler and tells me he is going to give me 10 shots across the ass for lying. I ran out of the classroom and never went back.

Since I was still under sixteen I had to sign up at another school. My probation officer got me into a pretty good high school, but school was the last thing on my mind. Again I never brought notebooks or pens. One teacher, Miss Smith, insisted I take notes one day. She gives me a sheet of paper and lends me a pen. There is no ink in the pen so she lets me fill the pen from her ink bottle. After I do so she tells me that will cost five cents for the ink, cause she has to buy the ink and it will teach me responsibility. I had about $130 I had stolen from a riding academy. One of the bills was a hundred dollar bill which I couldn't cash because I was too small. So I give it to her and tell her to take the five cents out and give me change. She was dumbfounded and the whole class laughed. Of course she didn't have change and she started blustering where did I get it from. I then gave her a $20 bill and again, she didn't have change. The class was in an uproar and the teacher was turning all colors, so then I pull out a dollar bill and like a real big shot I tell her "Keep the change." The class was completely disrupted now and when she calmed down a bit, she grabbed my ear and marched me to the principal. He asked me where I got the money and I quickly saw I could get myself in trouble, so I told him I stole it from my mother. He calls up my mother and tells her to come to the school. When she gets there and passes me sitting in the waiting room, on her way to the principal's office I jump up and yell, "Ma, I'm sorry I stole the $130 from your drawer," hoping she'll pick up the situation. Sure enough she tells the principal she did have that money in the drawer so he has to give it back to her. He tells me he doesn't want me back in school, so we leave. My mother gives me half the money and says she needs the rest. What could I say. At least the cops didn't get into it.

Me and a few others started robbing the fags downtown.

How we would work it is this. Since I was the youngest looking, I would stand in front of a restaurant in Times Square looking in and watching the people eat. In a few minutes, a fag would sidle up and ask me if I was hungry. I'd tell him yes but I have no money. Then he'd say if I came with him he would give me money. On the way to his place my friends who were following would jump him at the first dark alley. We made money like this just about every night.

We knew Times Square like the backs of our hands. There wasn't a movie we couldn't sneak into, whether through a side door or over the roofs. We were down there every night. My sisters were always asking me for money, and generally I'd give them some if I had it. A lot of times they wouldn't have anything to eat if I didn't have money. In that case I would go to the A & P and fill up a bag full of food and just walk out with it. As much as I gave my sisters, whenever I went to jail they very seldom wrote and never sent me any money.

I would do anything for kicks. We would hitch on a truck going upstate. The trucks used to have a little crib over the cab that would hold the rolled up canvas. We would climb up along the top of the truck and crawl into this crib. Many times I fell asleep up there. When I woke up I might be in Boston, or Maine, or somewhere else out of New York. If the cops got us first they would send us back to the City, otherwise we would hitch back. Jumping on the back of a truck was a common thing then. Today you don't see it at all. I use to dive off the Willis Ave. Bridge into the Harlem River. That was a damn good dive for a little kid. Or we would hold on to the side of a subway train and go from station to station.

One night I decide to sneak into the Roxy movie. I have a sure way to get in and my friend comes with me. As we are climbing up the fire escape we pass the girls' dressing room. The door is open and I see a pocketbook. We go in and all

24

the girls had left their pocketbooks in the dressing room while they went on stage. We start rifling them. My friend opens a door and a guard downstairs notices him and tells him to come down. The idiot goes down. I go down with him. The guard sees we are just kids so he puts his gun away. As he is searching my friend, I push him and he stumbles over a metal support. I push the door open and run. I look back and my friend is still standing there. Hoping he doesn't rat on me I go back to the neighborhood. Several days later he shows up. He swears he didn't rat on me.

The very next day my probation officer comes and gets me. He puts me in the Tombs, a men's detention prison, though I am not quite sixteen. Because of my age, I am not supposed to be there, but I didn't know it then. It was truly a horror. We were locked up 23 hours a day, and as bad as that was coming out for that one hour was even worse. There were a couple of guys there that were determined to rape me. They would grab me and start kissing me and feel my ass. I was terrified. Many times I tried to stay in my cell for that one hour, but the guards wouldn't let me. I think the only thing that saved me was that I looked only about thirteen years old. Some of the guys told the would-be rapists that because I was so young there would be a real big stink if they raped me and everybody might get in trouble.

Finally I go to court and the Legal Aid lawyer tells the judge he should parole me because I certainly don't belong in the Tombs. Fortunately the judge went along with it, and I was released until trial time. The judge tells me to behave myself and he might give me a break. I go back to the neighborhood and I see the fuck that ratted on me. I just tell him to stay away. I don't want to fight with him cause then I'll be in more trouble. They had brought him to children's court so he has nothing to worry about. I quit fucking around, no more stealing. I started shining shoes downtown and was

25

making money. I was scared to death of getting sent away. My probation officer wasn't too happy about me shining shoes—he'd rather I went to school regularly—but he figured as long as I was shining shoes all day, I wasn't doing any stealing.

One day I was shooting craps with the guys in the street. The fuck that ratted on me comes and starts playing. I told him to get the fuck out of here but his older brother was there so he figured he was safe. We started pushing each other around and I trip him and knock him down. He bangs his head on a milk crate and starts bleeding. They take him to the hospital and he gets stitched up. I go to court on my case the next week, and who shows up in court but him and his mother. He had his head completely bandaged. This is ridiculous because the last time I saw him he had only a small bandage covering a couple of stitches. His mother had put all that bandage over his head making it look like his whole head had been cut open. Then she gets up in front of the judge and starts lying that I had deliberately split her son's head open and I was a rotten kid and dangerous and a lot of other shit. The judge believes her nonsense and when I try to say something he cuts me off saying he tried to give me a break but he couldn't allow me to remain on the streets and he was going to send me some place for my own good. Meantime he sends me back to the Tombs, to await sentence. The ironic part of this is years later I find out I should never have allowed the Legal Aid lawyer to talk me into pleading guilty. All I had to do was deny being at the Roxy movie. The guard couldn't identify me and my friend's word wasn't enough to stand up in court. There was no way they could have found me guilty. But I didn't know it then and it cost me three years.

4

So I stood there and listened to the judge tell me he was going to help me get my life straightened out. He was going to sentence me to three years in a State Correctional Institution. Although the name sounded imposing, it was really a place where I would be helped: I would get psychiatric care and I could learn a trade. I'd be out in the country and I would be released in a year. In a very fatherly manner he told me if he allowed me to return to the streets, I would wind up in State Prison. (What a laugh.) And that though I might not appreciate it now, I would later on. I have often wondered if he really believed that shit he was telling me.

We pulled up to Elmira, after a long train ride, handcuffed, none of us over seventeen, and I barely sixteen. As soon as we went through the front doors, I knew this was going to be no picnic. The guards were big, and their manner forceful. We were given bologna sandwiches on stale bread along with a rule book, assigned cells and told study the rule book. There was a window in the back of each cell, stone walls, and a steel door with a small opening. I lay on the bed with a lump in my throat, not wanting to cry, but scared to death. I remember thinking back over my life as I lay there wondering how the fuck I got here. It seemed as if I had spent my whole life in a cell or institution of some kind, being ordered around and talked to crudely. I lay awake most of the night, crying off and on. I wished I could die right there.

The cell door opened in the morning and I looked down the tier. It was a long cell block with four tiers facing each other. Except for skin color, each boy looked almost identical —gray pants and shirts, short haircuts, fearful looks and black smiles on faces.

The guards quickly established their authority, and showed where their heads were at. They lined us up and told us we better keep in step: no talking, no smoking, and when we go into the mess hall, keep our eyes straight ahead, eat all we take, and when we return to our tiers march straight to our cells, face the door and wait for it to open. I am sure many of our fears would have been allayed if only one of these guards could have spoken in a more humane manner. Here we were, a bunch of scared kids, living in cells like animals, knowing we'd have to be here for a couple of years, and from the guards' attitudes we quickly felt no one gave a damn if we lived or died.

Since there was little recreation or socializing, I had no idea what was in store for me later on. I was the smallest person there and comments were thrown at me about my "fine body" and what a sweet ass I had. "I'd sure like to fuck you." This is what I had to listen to most of the day. I didn't really know what to do about it. Frequently the guards heard the remarks and all they did was laugh, so I knew I couldn't expect much help from them. I went through this shit each time we came out of our cells, either in orientation classes, the clinic, the mess hall or the 45-minute exercise period. I kept to myself, and outwardly ignored the remarks.

I dreaded the long hours in my cell, and dreaded coming

28

out of the cell. I wanted to die but was too afraid to think of suicide. Eventually one guy did grab my ass. I turned and pushed him away, and he started grappling with me. Seconds later the guards came running saying, "Break up the fighting." They slapped and punched us around and marched us to one of the strip cells. These cells were stripped of all but a toilet and sink. Nothing but stone walls and stone floors. There we had to stay until we saw the Deputy Warden who was also the disciplinarian. He would decide what punishment to mete out. We were served two meals a day, breakfast and supper on a tray. We had to sleep on the bare floors. We were not allowed to read or smoke or do anything. Just sit on the floor or the toilet, or walk up and down. To give you just a vague idea of what living in a cell is like, go in your bathroom, which is about the size of a cell, six feet wide, nine feet long. Try to block out the tub and medicine chest, stay in there for a while and visualize living in that space for years. Just imagine staying in there all day, and curling up on the floor to sleep at night.

Lots of thoughts went through my head. Was I some kind of animal? What did I do wrong when I was born? What the fuck was wrong with me? Was I hated this much by God? I was filled with pity for myself, and there was no one to talk to. If only someone cared.

Two days later we were thrown some clothes, and told we were going to court. That's what it was called when you were up on an infraction. The guard told us we were charged with fighting. "Fighting." All I did was push him away from grabbing my ass. Waiting outside the P.K.'s office (the Deputy Warden's other title was Principal Keeper) the fellow that grabbed my ass sidled up to me and warned me I better tell the P.K. I pushed him first, or else he would get me. More fear came over me. When was this going to stop? I knew if I said I had started the fight, I would get the most punishment. Yet I felt too embarrassed to tell the P.K. that the other boy grabbed my ass. He might think I was a sissy or faggot. So when I was called in and asked what happened I refused to say anything. The other boy said I had pushed him for no reason. Before I had a chance to say anything even if I had wanted to, the P.K. turned to me and said, "So you are in this place three days, and already you think you are a tough guy. Well, we'll see how tough you are—ten days strip cell." This meant I had to spend ten days in the stripped cell without coming out. The other boy was let go with a suspended sentence. I walked back to the cell with my head fucked up. Ten days seemed like an eternity in that cell. I didn't know how I had survived the two previous days.

My clothes were taken from me and I was left with shorts, a tee shirt and a pair of socks. As the steel door closed on me everything went out of my body. It just felt numb. Couldn't anybody understand I wasn't a tough guy? I didn't want to be left alone. Feelings of hate came over me. I hated everybody: my parents, the judge, God, the guards, the other inmates, the whole damn world. They didn't care about me and I don't care about them. Fuck everybody. And then I started to cry. Disgust came over me for being such a weakling and crying. I tried to stop but couldn't.

Since that time, I've spent a lot of time in punishment cells and suffered much pain, both physical and mental, but I have always felt that those ten days were the worst of my life.

After the ten days were up, I was released back to my tier. My next infraction came when I refused to let the doctor give me a needle. At that time I had a morbid fear of needles, and his machinelike manner of giving the needles didn't help any. One would imagine that at least a doctor would be a sympathetic person in a prison, but with the exception of perhaps two prison doctors the rest were every bit as rotten as the guards. Absolutely no humane feeling. Hasty diagnosis, inadequate and improper medication and you better not talk back. So there I was, back before the P.K. I tried to explain to him my fear of needles, that I wasn't trying to be a wise guy, but he just cut in and said 30 days Keep Lock to give you a chance to think about it. This meant I had to spend the next thirty days locked in my cell, coming out just once a week to take a shower. Well at least I had a bed this time. A few fellows on the tier would sneak me a magazine when they came by.

I survived the next three months there by talking seldom, keeping to myself, and having a blank stare on my face. This soon caused the guards to consider me a cocky, smug person. Little did they know or even care, how scared and confused I was inside.

I knew it was just a matter of time until someone "tested" me. Since I didn't fight back or reply to any of the "Sweet Boy" comments thrown at me, some of the inmates were getting braver and trying to press me more, telling me what they would do to me if they caught me alone. I was terrified coming out of the cell each morning. Finally I was assigned to mop up the gallery. As I was filling up the bucket in the slop sink room, two guys grabbed me and one pressed his cock against my ass. The other one was trying to kiss me. Instinctively I threw my arms around, and the can of soap powder I had in my hand went in the face of one of them. He screamed as it went in his eyes.

The guards quickly came and broke us up. The one boy was rushed to the infirmary and the other said all they did was ask me for some soap to clean their cells, and I told them no, go fuck yourself. I denied this futilely because all the guards wanted to believe was that I threw soap powder in someone's eyes, perhaps blinding them. They began punching me around, and when I fell, they just kicked me and said get up. I was soon a bloody mess. They dragged me to strip cell. I lay on the floor, not knowing how bad my wounds

31

were. I just couldn't believe what happened. What the fuck did I do? One minute I was getting ready to mop the floor with nothing on my mind, the next minute here I am in strip cell, all beat up. This couldn't be real. This would all get straightened out, and they would realize they were wrong for beating me up. A doctor came after a few hours, looked at my wounds in a half-ass manner, said nothing serious there, and left. I had to wash the blood off myself. I curled up in the corner and cried myself to sleep.

The next morning I went to the P.K.'s office. The guards, in an attempt to justify their beating me, backed the other boys' story. At that point I learned there was never any sense trying to explain to the P.K. one's side of an infraction. The guards were always right. And the P.K. didn't particularly care anyway. The P.K. sent me back to the strip cell until the next day. He wanted to first find out how serious the soap powder damage was.

I went back to the cell totally disgusted. Fuck it all, man, I don't care what happens to me anymore. I wish I could have really felt that way, but I knew it was just false bravado. What if I really blinded the guy. I knew I would be brought to court outside and given a new sentence. What a rotten mother-fucking world. Just at that moment my cell door opened. It was time for supper and my tray was being handed to me. The guard stands by each cell as the tray is handed in. I looked up and the bastard handing me the tray was a friend of the other two. He pursed his lips at me as if throwing a kiss. This was one of the ways they had in trying to break down a guy they want to fuck. Any time they saw a guy who was young and good looking, they would purse their lips at them as if kissing them. Anger boiled up inside me, and all the frustration inside me pushed out. I slapped the tray up into his face. I was sick of all this bullshit. I screamed, "Leave me the fuck alone." The inmate jumped out of the way, his black face whitened by the macaroni. I heard the guard yelling, and the next thing I knew, several of them were in my cell, punching at me. I lay there hurting all night, wondering what was going to happen to me. Of course the guard's report mentioned nothing of the other fellow provoking me. He couldn't have seen it.

When I went to see the P.K. next day, he had both infractions before him. His anger was such, you would think I had hit him personally or something. He told me I thought I was a cocky son-of-a-bitch, and I had a chip on my shoulder, and he was going to knock it off. So he sentenced me to strip cell indefinitely. This meant I would be let out only when he decided to let me out. I was brought back to the cell. The chief clerk was there and told me to sign a piece of paper, and he had two letters in his hand. The paper I had to sign was that the letters were received. I signed the paper and was then told I could not receive the letters because the girl that wrote them was not on my approved correspondence list. I hadn't yet received mail from anyone. When I saw the letters were from Barbara, my girl friend, I asked him to at least let me read them and I would give them back to him. He refused. Desolation came over me. The one person who cared for me was rejected by the institution. I was alone, completely alone. What more could happen to me?

The days dragged by in the strip cell. Each day seemed like a year. My feelings were those of utter hopelessness. My anger and hate began building up inside and there was no outlet. After about 28 days, the P.K. called me to his office, and said if I wanted a bed to sleep on I would have to write him an interview slip asking for one. He wanted me to beg. Well, fuck him. I decided right then, I would never ask him for a bed. Immediately, I felt better. At least now I was fighting back. I felt more like a man. Perhaps ten days later, a Captain came to my cell, and asked me if I wanted an interview slip to write to the P.K. asking for a bed. I told him no. I would never ask for one. He said, "We'll see." More days passed, again I was asked if I wanted a bed. I replied that if they wanted to give me one, okay, but I certainly wasn't going to ask for one. This attitude further angered the guards. They began giving me less food, the coffee in the morning would be cold, and rather than the allotted time in the shower, I would barely get soaped up and they would tell me the shower is over. It is almost impossible to conceive how these animalistic guards could treat another human being, much less a kid.

I must have been in the strip cell, sleeping on the floor for something like 80-odd days. This was far longer than anyone else ever had to do. Finally the P.K. called me to his office. In a surprisingly nicer manner, he asked me how I was doing, and did I think I could adjust to the prison rules, and that wise guys in prison did a hard bit. His manner completely threw me off. I expected him to rant and rave, and I was prepared for that, but when he started to talk nice, a lump formed in my throat. I wanted to trust somebody so badly, and tell them all I was a scared lonely guy. I almost started crying. Then he said if I wanted to fill out the request slip for the bed, rather than me fill it out in my cell and have it go through the regular channels, I could fill it out there in his office and he would grant the request for the bed. The son-of-a-bitch. He was still going to make me beg for the bed. I told him, I had promised myself never to ask for that bed, and I couldn't go back on myself. Reverting to his normal self he started ranting and raving and threatening me, and promised to "Fix me." He then ordered me out of his office. Several days later I was transferred to Coxsackie. This was a prison for youthful offenders. They called it a reformatory, whatever that means, but it was worse than any State Prison I later did time in.

34

5

So that was my introduction to the New York State penal system. At no point in that institution nor any other institution I went to, did anyone ever try to understand what makes a person act as he does. At no time was decency and kindness used as a tool to reach someone. We were all just animals and second-grade humans, to be controlled only through the use of clubs and punishment.

Looking back, years later, on my time spent in that strip cell, refusing to ask for a bed, I learned the P.K. had had to transfer me out. He saw that I was not going to give in and realistically speaking he couldn't keep me in strip cell for the rest of my sentence. The only other solution was that he would either have to give me a bed, which would mean I won in standing up to him, or ship me out. Naturally he did the latter. The report he sent along on me didn't give me much of a chance in Coxsackie.

The P.K. in charge there, in this youthful institution, was one of the three most sadistic officials I ever encountered. The fact that we were human beings, the fact that none of us were hardened criminals, and that most of us were under nineteen years of age meant nothing to him. Judging by his attitude toward us one might think we were all in prison for murder and/or rape.

It was while in this institution that I began to change. Any decent thoughts I may have had I started pushing to the back of my mind. I began learning how to be slick, how to scheme. I learned about various crimes and how to commit them. I learned how to be sneaky. And I learned violence is the only way to command respect. Violence is a way of life in prison. It is introduced by the guards the moment you enter the prison. They tell you they're the bosses and you better listen to them, banging their sticks for emphasis. Violence is carried on through the institution by the guards. Practically every day, in this youthful institution someone was getting either beaten badly or slapped around. I had decided that I wasn't going to allow any of the inmates to fuck with me this time. I was going to establish that I was no sissy or fag. I realized that because of my small physical size I wasn't going to win any of the fights, but I figured if they knew I would fight back eventually they would leave me alone.

The first night in the institution, in the mess hall for the evening meal, a big black grabbed my ass. I threw my tray at him and jumped on him wrestling him to the ground. I knew that if I ever let him up he would beat me badly. We were quickly surrounded by guards. Fighting in prison is serious, but it is even worse when you fight in the mess hall or auditorium. This is where the inmates are congested together and there is always a chance inmates might prevent the guards from using their clubs on another inmate. There are tear gas bombs in the ceilings of both places. The guard in the observation tower just has to push the button and these bombs fall and explode.

36

I and the other inmate were beaten and literally dragged to the punishment cells. There we waited until the P.K. called us to court two days later. If that bastard had any humaneness, or sense of caring, he could have easily seen what the fight was all about. All he had to do was to look at the size of the other guy. That together with the fact that this was my first day in the institution and I certainly couldn't have any beefs against this guy, showed there was only one reason for this fight. But the fact that I started this fight, plus the fact that I started it in the mess hall, was all the bastard cared about. Ten days strip cell on bread and water: this was his sentence. The other fellow was given ten days no privileges. This meant loss of movies and yard. So again I was the bad guy.

Strip cell here was just like the other strip cell. The bread and water punishment meant that I would be given instead of a meal, two slices of bread in the morning and two slices of bread in the evening. That was all I would be given to eat. Every third day, because the state rule decreed it, I would be given a half meal. I spent Christmas in that strip cell on bread and water. As I looked out the window, I could see two or three houses. They were lit up with lights. I felt sick. I had never experienced a good Christmas, one with love and good feelings. I cried hard, and long, and it was the last time I cried in twenty years.

While I was in that strip cell, I decided how I was going to do my time. Since no one cared what the real me was like, and all it did was get me in trouble, I was going to present a new me. I was not going to let others know how weak and scared I was inside. I was going to adopt a cold outward tough-guy stance. A man can endure a physical beating. I mean of course it hurts for a while, but at least you get over it. But the mental beating and pain that is constantly administered if you are in any sense a sensitive person, is the pain that really hurts for a long, long time. Before I left that place any decency I had was pushed down deep inside me. I began to grow into that cold callous person that I presented externally.

In that cell I learned how to go to sleep with my belly aching from hunger. I would save the two slices of bread I received in the morning. When I received the two in the evening I would knead the four of them together into one big hard ball. Then just before laying down to go to sleep, I would take big bites of the ball and swallow them without chewing them. These lumps would then go into my stomach and I would feel full. The trick was to go to sleep before the bread digested. Sometimes I would put a little toothpaste on the bread to flavor it.

Those three years in the "youthful institution" were the worst three years of my life. I think back now and wonder how I ever survived. How any of us ever survived. No wonder most of our state prison inmates are graduates of these "youthful reformatories."

I learned a lot while there. Besides learning about various crimes, I learned how to do time. That it is you against them. Them meaning the officials. I learned that a violent person gains more respect. I learned there is an unwritten axiom in all N.Y. prisons, "Fuck, but don't fight." In other words, the officials don't mind too much if a boy gets raped. That can be hushed up. But if one inmate hurts another to the extent of one having to be hospitalized in an outside hospital, the officials don't like outsiders knowing what's going on in the prison.

In the upstate institutions, it is almost unreal, the intense dislike the officials have for the inmates. In their eyes, we are city slickers: thieves, rapists or murderers, and/or wops, niggers, spicks, Irish bastards. I would say this holds true for 90 percent of all the officials I encountered. You are made to feel subhuman from the moment you walk into the prison. And it's ingenious, the methods of punishment they can dream up. It's not bad enough to lock you in a cell behind 40-foot walls. Oh no, they have become very innovative in their way of punitive treatment once they have got you behind these walls. Strip cell, bread and water, keeping you locked in your cell for six months or more, loss of mail privileges, loss of visits, making you march in close order all day under a blazing sun, putting you in a cell with nothing but a sink and toilet, and then flooding it with six to eight inches of water, handing you a rag the size of a washcloth and telling you when you mop up the water you can sleep on a dry floor. Man has excelled in the area of creating newer and better weapons of killing other humans, along with inflicting more and more ways of punishment. We must certainly hate each other.

Almost immediately after being released from the punishment cell, I got into more trouble. They had me down as a wise guy because I wouldn't kowtow to them. Though I was a scared and frightened boy, I was determined not to compromise myself. I wasn't going to show anything other than my dislike for them. To get on the hacks' good side some inmates butter them up and con the hack into thinking they are not such bad guards.

During this period there was this one big black that was really fucking with me. Every time he saw me he would throw kisses, and rub his dick, and tell me he was going to get my ass. I knew I had to do something. But what? I damn sure couldn't beat him. I'd stay up almost all night thinking about this bastard and dream up a million ways to get him. I hated him with a passion. He was really making my time miserable. I finally realized the only way to straighten the situation out with him and at the same time let everyone else know I wasn't pussy was to really hurt him. And to do this I would need a weapon. "Piping a guy," which means hitting a guy over the head with a pipe, is a pretty common thing in prison. Until this moment I couldn't even picture myself hurting someone like that; I didn't even believe I was capable of doing something like that. But I started thinking of it each night. In my frenzied anger and hate towards this guy I fantasized constantly of "piping" him. There was no other way, I told myself; because I was letting him get away with fucking with me, others figured I was an easy thing and would fuck with me also. I was desperate. I had to do something. Anything was better than this.

The next time I saw him I told him to meet me in the bathroom at a certain time. His eyes lit up. Generally when you told someone to meet you in the shithouse, it meant you were going to rumble. But he was so sure of himself, knowing I was no match for him, that even if I did try to fight with him, he could overpower and rape me. I took the iron pipe off the mop wringer and got to the shithouse about ten minutes earlier than I said. I hid in one of the cubicles with my feet on the toilet so he couldn't see any part of me. I heard him come in. I peeked through the cubicle door and saw him standing there facing the outer door, as cocky as hell. I was shaking frantically, not because of fear but at what I was about to do. I had psyched myself into doing this and now I wasn't sure I could go through with it. I was also worried about how hard to hit him. If I hit him too easy he would turn around and kill me. If I hit him too hard I might kill him. Then I began thinking how this nigger was trying to fuck me, and how he made every day miserable for me. Fuck it, I said. I pushed the cubicle door open slowly, took two quick steps and swung the pipe straight at the back of his head. It made a crunch and immediately blood spurted out. He slumped to the floor. Shit, did I kill him? I stood there with the pipe in my hand, not knowing what to do. If I had had any sense, or

40

if I was a bit more callous, I would have just wiped the pipe off and snuck out of the bathroom. But I hadn't yet reached that state of insensibility. I don't know how long I stood there before someone opened the door to come in. They saw him laid out on the floor, a real bloody mess. I heard them yell and pretty soon the door was crowded with hacks. For a moment I was forgotten. All eyes were on him. I was close to throwing up. I never saw so much blood in my life. I was sure he was dead. They got him out of there on a stretcher. The next thing I know I was getting beat from one end of the hall to the other. They dragged me up to segregation, made me strip and they formed a circle around me and beat me with their clubs. When I fell they kicked at me.

I awoke in a strip cell. I was hurting badly, and there was blood all over me. I just didn't care. I hated the whole world. On one hand I felt good at hitting that motherfucker, that's what he gets for fucking with a man, but at the same time I began thinking what would happen to me if I had killed him. Oh shit, I wish I was dead. I was tired of people fucking with me. I couldn't put up with this life much longer. It wasn't worth the hassle. The next day the doctor came to check for broken bones, stitched me up and said I was okay.

I lay in the cell for days not knowing what was happening. Then word came up via the grapevine; the cat wasn't going to die. There was talk about bringing me to an outside court and charging me with deadly assault. I had accomplished one thing. I had gained the others' respect. The inmates in segregation were on my side. Their attitudes had changed. I was an okay guy. The P.K. sentenced me to segregation indefinite. The first 30 days I had no bed. After that I was given a bed. There were 24 cells on each side, with a small opening in the door. Through this we would talk with fellows across the way, using sign language. We would get some string, either from the mattress or a thin strip of the sheet. This we would lower to the floor below us and the guy underneath would tie some cigarettes or tobacco and papers on it. Occasionally one of us would get caught and get an ass whipping, and our beds taken from us. We never minded this too much. It was worth taking the chance because it was helping us to survive. If one didn't rebel by breaking the rules you became a broken person. You had to keep fighting back just to tell yourself you were a man, and they weren't going to break you. Too many people came out of prison completely broken and useless. I didn't want that to happen to me. I was a man I kept telling myself, but inside I wondered.

I was up in segregation thirteen months which was an unusually long time. Every time they caught me breaking the rules, they added more time to my stay up there. The P.K. told me quite frankly he didn't care if I spent my whole three years up there. The only thing they let you have to read was the Bible. Shit, I must have read it a dozen times. Some of it I found interesting, especially the parts where the man "knew" the woman. I found some pretty sexy parts in there. The Song of Solomon was considered pretty erotic by all of us and never failed to arouse us sexually. I masturbated several times a day reading the Bible. Occasionally I got a letter from my parents telling me to be a good boy and do everything the officials tell me. I had written my mother telling her to come up, that it was an emergency. I wanted to tell her about all the shit happening to me. What she did instead was to call up the P.K. and ask what was happening with me. He told her some shit about me and pretty soon I got a letter from her telling me the P.K. was a very nice man and spoke so nice to her and that I should do as he tells me. God, what a bitch. I wondered if she was drunk when she

Several guys tried suicide while in segregation. Some faked it to get sent to a mental hospital, and some were for

42

real. One fellow died while I was up there. He had hung himself when he heard the hack making his rounds. But the cop had just walked by his cell. They found him dead hours later. I was in a pretty depressed state. I kept thinking about my past life and what the future held for me. I still had two years left of my sentence and I couldn't picture doing it in segregation. And even when I got out, what was in store for me? Just more brutality, more suffering, and still no one to care for me.

I began thinking about death a lot. It fascinated me. It couldn't be any worse than life. I didn't believe in that shit about Heaven or Hell. You were dead, period. Then I would push it out of my mind, but late at night when I couldn't sleep, it would come to me again. Then I thought of what happened to the guys that had cut their wrists with a piece of glass or hanged themselves. When the hacks found them they beat the hell out of them. Of course all the hacks could think of was that these guys were just faking it looking for sympathy.

I just lay there day after long day. I later found out the law stated we were to get an hour exercise each day, but at that time who knew anything about such a law. I used to masturbate so much my dick would get blisters on it. There was nothing else to do, and coming was the only good feeling, though it ended so quickly.

One night I decided fuck it. I wasn't going to let this shit go on any longer. Without even thinking about it, like a robot, I made a noose out of the sheet climbed up on the window and jumped off. All I knew was that I didn't want to be a part of this world. I came to with several hacks around me. I heard someone saying, "He's okay now." Someone else was saying, "The son of a bitch should have done a better job." Remember they are talking about a seventeen-year-old person. This was their callous animalistic attitude. And these

43

are our keepers! For some reason I didn't get beaten. I was put in a strip cell completely naked. The next day a bug doctor came to see me. I decided I was going to play crazy. It couldn't be much worse in a state hospital. I told him I didn't care about living and that I would do it again. A couple of days later I was sent to Matteawan State Hospital. When I heard the news I sure felt relieved to be leaving this hell.

6

During the ride to Matteawan, my mind was filled with confused feelings. On the one hand, I was glad to be out of solitary confinement, but on the other hand, I was also terrified of just what I had gotten myself into. The two hacks from Coxsackie driving me to Matteawan, were telling each other stories they had heard regarding the nut house, and what a real hell hole it was. They were deliberately telling these stories so as to get me all panicky and up tight. They were succeeding too, because just by the way they had me shackled convinced me I was going to some kind of special terrible place. Both my feet were chained and my hands were cuffed to a wide leather belt locked to my waist. It was about an hour's ride and I wondered just what was so terrible about me that at the age of seventeen I had to be bound in such a manner. Was I really that vicious? Were they afraid I was some type of an animal that would devour them if they treated me less severe? What was so different about me that caused people not to understand that all I wanted was some concern, someone to take an interest in me that I was alive and not much different from other young kids?

The grounds surrounding Matteawan belied the conditions inside. Lots of green grass bordered by a high chain fence. Certainly an improvement over Coxsackie where the yard was surrounded by corridors and buildings, and one seldom saw grass and fields. Then my eyes turned to the building itself. A bleak, brick, immense structure. The depressing, dismal appearance of the place fitted perfectly with the atmosphere of the inside.

I was quickly hustled out of the car and into the building, the hacks gloating over my tripping on the foot shackles. I had approximately a two-minute interview with the receiving psychiatrist, signed in and was sent to the receiving ward. Ward A. Walking through the ward to the Head Charge's office (he is the cop who is in charge of the ward) was quite a shocking experience. I saw grown men walking around as if in some kind of horror movie, like zombies. I saw men talking to themselves, or to the walls or furniture. Other men were sitting in chairs as if they had been there so long they had grown roots to the chair, just sitting and staring out, without moving a muscle. I passed some small rooms and saw others completely covered with some kind of dirty canvas, which I later found out to be restraining sheets. They literally tied one immobile, except for being able to turn the head from side to side. Still others were walking around with straitjackets on.

I later found out through observation and personal experience that these jackets and restraining sheets weren't used for the patients' benefit. Rather they were used for punishment. For any infraction of the rules, or just on an officer's whim, a patient would be tightly bound in the jacket or sheet. The officer would force a patient to his knees, put his foot on the patient's back, and then pull as tightly as possible the

46

two ropes that forced the arms to be pulled around the patient's back. Immediately the rough canvas would scrape against the elbow and soon the elbows would be extremely sore and bloody. A man would be forced to stay in one of these for anywhere from a couple of hours to several days. This jacket would sometimes be taken off only to allow the man to eat. Otherwise someone would have to feed him. He had to sleep and piss and shit with this on.

A man in a straitjacket was entirely at the other patients' mercy. By this I mean if some patient went berserk violently, the man in the straitjacket had best hope he wasn't around, because he had no way to defend himself. I remember a very tragic incident occurring in Bellevue psycho ward, where an alcoholic, thirty-two years old, was tied tightly to a bed with a restraining sheet. In the same room was a young boy, picked up wandering the streets, completely out of it. Well this boy went absolutely berserk and attacked the alcoholic who was tied down. The screams penetrated every hall and corridor in the psycho wards. Before being pulled out of the room he had completely bitten off the testicles of the alcoholic, who was defenseless because of being bound. Neither of these fellows were in the criminal side of the psycho ward, but the boy was immediately brought down to our ward. Before being transferred to an insane asylum this boy bit off the finger of a nurse's aide who was in the process of feeding him. So you can easily see the dangers of being helpless in a psycho ward.

As I said the use of the straitjacket or the restraining sheet was for punishment purposes. I was, during my stay in Matteawan, put in a straitjacket several times either for a fight or some other infraction, or by some hack who just disliked me.

Getting back to my first day in Matteawan, I was ushered into the Charge's office. There I was told the rules and proce-

47

dure in no uncertain terms. In the room were two officers and a young girl. I wondered what a young very pretty girl was doing there; I was soon to find out. I was told to strip for a search, and then to shower. Noticing my hesitation to strip with the girl there, the officer then told me, "Don't worry about Jimmy, he's probably got a bigger cock than you have." Which incidentally happened to be the case. Anyway I was really knocked for a loop, cause this kid was beautiful, with makeup on and plucked eyebrows, and even wearing a feminine shirt. Seeing my awkwardness, the cops got a big laugh and furthered the joke by telling Jimmy to help me take a shower. I was completely infatuated with Jimmy. To me, he was as pretty a girl as any girl could be. I later found out Jimmy was one of those rare individuals that are born with both male and female organs, and was a true hermaphrodite.

Jimmy took a liking to me right away and tried to give me a complete rundown on the place: who to avoid, which hacks were really rotten, and just about everything necessary to get me over the shock of the place. The food was practically inedible, most meals smelled so bad and looked even worse that the only ones that ate such meals were the real nuts who were incapable of knowing the difference of foods. I quickly learned the ropes, stayed by myself, except for rapping with Jimmy. I really thought of Jimmy as a girl and I was getting uptight sexually. So far there hadn't been a place for me to get him really alone. My movements were very much restricted, since this was the receiving ward, where all the newcomers had to stay put. Jimmy, of course could move around, since he had been there for some time. Plus most of the cops dug Jimmy, because he could do a lot of favors for them, such as swagging food, money, etc.

I learned Jimmy's story one night and it was a very pathetic one. His parents brought him up as a girl, and then gave him up to foster parents. They too, brought him up as a girl, and in truth, he was far more girl than boy. His skin was smoother than most girls, no beard, and he had a very much female voice. In school he became very confused and unsure of his role in life. He had no friends at all, wasn't allowed in the girls' bathroom or locker room, and he dreaded going into the boys' toilet. He soon started playing hookey, got into a lot of trouble over this, and soon he ran away. An elderly man picked him up hitchhiking, took him to Florida, bought him women's clothes and sold his services to many of his well-to-do friends.

Eventually Jimmy got picked up by the police in Florida and was sent back to New York, where the courts ruled him a wayward minor, only because his foster parents wanted nothing more to do with him, and his delinquency at school. He was judged a wayward minor without even committing a crime. He was just seventeen when the judge committed him to Elmira Reformatory, reception center—a real heartless bastard that had no idea of his responsibilities as a judge. It is exactly people like this that cause the destruction of many lives. Picture placing a female in a male prison and left to the mercy of the inmates, who haven't seen a female in years. That is just what the judge, probation officer and warden did. Each hour there was a living hell for Jimmy. I know from personal experience some of what he went through, and I certainly didn't look like a girl nor was as defenseless as he. Jimmy attempted suicide shortly after. He placed his mattress and some newspapers by his cell door, set them afire, and then hung himself with torn sheets. By the time the cops opened the cell door and got through the flames, Jimmy was close to death. A few days later they sent him to Matteawan. At one point he attempted suicide in Matteawan. He just couldn't cope with being a female in a men's institution.

Eventually Jimmy learned to survive through his

femininity. He won most of the hacks over, and this caused the inmates to think twice about fucking with him. The cops only protected him because of what he could do for them. Jimmy let me know from the start that he wasn't a whore. True, he made a lot of money there but he did it without having to give up his body. Many of the patients that were well off would send him money from their wards. You have to understand most of these people were sick, and really believed Jimmy was their woman, even though they couldn't get near him. They would also pay someone in the kitchen to give Jimmy special meals; at times there were perhaps 50 guys all paying to give Jimmy special meals. I started working in the kitchen and soon I was the guy getting the money for Jimmy, which I split with him. I began courting Jimmy just as I would a woman, and I actually thought of him as a girl. Kissing him was sweeter than any kissing I had known. Ultimately, we became very close lovers, and I believe I truly loved Jimmy. Even now I have a tendency to refer to Jimmy as HER.

After I was there a short while, a guy came in that had stabbed several people in the streets for no reason. He just flipped his lid, and was sent to Matteawan. He was black, and because of this and his crime, before any of the officers even saw him three or four hacks from my ward, upon learning he was coming in that day, decided to break him in right. They were going to "teach this nigger a lesson." I heard the whole conversation and wondered just how bad a beating he was to get. As familiar as I was with the sadistic ways of these bastards, what they did was still shocking. As soon as he entered the ward, several cops grabbed him and beat him savagely, calling him nigger, etc. They then threw him down four flights of stairs, placed his arm between two steps and one of the cops very deliberately jumped on his arm. Needless to say, his arm was shattered. He was given a quick patch up job and placed in the locked cells. These were cells in a back ward, that were used for punishment and also for the very violent cases. Many of the men in those cells, bolted with double doors, were locked there for ten or fifteen years. They were utterly forgotten men, their food was pushed in under the door, their baths consisted of being hosed down when the cop felt like it. A man placed in those cells was in effect condemned to death. Germany's concentration camps? Russia's Siberia? Japanese prison camps? No! New York State's System! I remember seeing one of these rooms. There was actually a depression in the wooden floor where a man had walked back and forth for years and years. You could see where he made his turn at each end of the cell. I did my time there, always walking as if on eggs.

I quickly realized beatings, cripplings and death were ever present and real. There was no one to appeal to. The only excuse the cops need give was "Injury (or death) caused while being restrained." I had several fights at first, but quickly they learned I was not to be considered fair game by the wolves, and that as soon as we were allowed out of the straitjackets, I would attack the man while he was asleep. There was an unwritten policy among the hacks: fuck but don't fight. This meant they would overlook homosexual activities, which occurred quite openly, but they would not tolerate fighting for any reason, including protecting oneself. I guess the cops felt anyone inflicting pain on someone else was infringing on their (the cops') territory.

I went to work in the kitchen because one could go crazy hanging around on the ward all day with absolutely nothing to do after cleanup was over in the morning. There were big heavy chairs all around the walls of the ward, and each patient was assigned a chair. On some wards, patients had to sit in these chairs all day continuously, having to raise their hands if they wanted to go to the toilet. This was a routine men did day after day, week after week, month after month, and some for years. This was truly the land of the living dead. Because I wasn't crazy and learned to scheme very quickly, I was soon gaining many of the better favors in the place, such as special food, clothes, liquor, and pot when I wanted it. Much of the money I made from my deal with Jimmy I bought favors with, and I gambled with the rest. I had a natural knack with cards, and generally won.

Soon a big-time bookie asked me to work for him, picking up bets, and he would set up games with the hacks for me, and he would back me. Most of the cops gambled and bet on the horses or ball games. All their bets would be placed with Mendy. In fact many of the civilians in town were giving their bets to cops that were friends of theirs to place the bet with Mendy. Mendy was there, as were so many others, because they had feigned insanity or paid their way to get sent to Matteawan rather than face their charges in court. It was common knowledge that if you did some time in Matteawan, depending on the seriousness of the charge, you would get a big break when you went back and faced your charge. Most likely you would get off. Working with Mendy took a lot of cops off my back, because there were few cops that wanted to buck Mendy over some petty bullshit. He had too many things going, all of which meant more money for the controlling cops.

I needed a someone like Mendy, because I just couldn't play up to the hacks. I still showed hostility toward them and wouldn't play up to them as they thought I should. Mendy convinced me I should at least not provoke trouble with them, and though I might hate them, never show it. In this manner I could get a lot more from them, including their money. By this he meant I would soon be asked to play regularly in their nightly card games and if I used my head I could fleece them in that manner, which I did. At times I had well over $500 in my pocket, more than I had when I was out. This satisfied all my needs except freedom. They had women patients working in the laundry, and though they were in another building, I could pay my way to the laundry, give the cop in charge of the laundry $20, and he would give me a contraceptive and I could take any girl that was willing behind one of the machines and fuck her over a laundry bag. This was a common practice which only slowed up when one of the girls became pregnant.

Things were going smoothly for me, I never gave too much thought to the future, not wanting to be reminded of the terrible times I had before. I lived for the day only, each day. My parents came up once, but it was a bad scene. I couldn't stand the sight of them. My girl friend came up occasionally—I think for the money I gave her—and I would bang her in the bathroom before she left. She would bring me booze but I didn't dig the stuff too tough, and I had a better drug connection on the inside than she had on the outside.

One time in the mess hall, I had some cornflakes and bananas which I had bought. I put some of each in my bowl and as I was pouring in the milk, I saw out of the corner of my eye the fellow next to me using my cornflakes. If he had asked, I would have given him some, but I got very angry seeing him just take them. I turned and asked him what the fuck he was doing and prepared myself to take a swing at him. His reaction stopped me dead. He turned and looked me right in the eye with a cold blank look and said that they weren't mine but God's, and God gives these things to everybody. Brother, he meant it, and I quickly saw this guy was out of it, and completely insane. I made sure never to sit next to him again.

I stayed high a lot from pot that was either smuggled in or bought from one of the cops, and also began using cocaine fairly regularly. Though there was no coke in the nearby town where the cops lived, there were several cops that went to New York and would look up a connection that an inmate gave him to bring back some coke or heroin. For this the cop would generally receive $100 for himself. My needs were pretty much fulfilled. The excitement I craved was constant. Gambling which always thrilled me, getting high, and also walking a thin line in my relations with the cops. And also my relations with Jimmy which most everyone envied. There were other female impersonators in the place, but none half as beautiful as Jimmy.

After my ward went to the yard, a very small one, the ward below us would go. This ward was filled with old insane men, with no families or friends to look after them, so they had no cigarettes. All the cigarette butts we left in the yard were like gold to them. They would be brought to the door of the yard, and the hacks would get out of the way, because once the yard door was opened, it was bedlam. Imagine about 150 men trampling each other in their mad rush to be first out in the yard, to get at the butts laying around on the ground. If any were unfortunate enough to fall they would be trampled by all those behind. The hacks always got a big laugh out of this.

Another time I saw a man go berserk on the ward. Not hurting anyone, just screaming and going into fits. When the hacks attacked him he broke loose and with superhuman strength began throwing chairs at them. As I said these were big heavy chairs, designed just so that they couldn't be used as weapons. The cops quickly got out the high-pressure water hose and turned the water on full force. They were very skillful at using this and in truth they delighted in their ability to aim the water in such a manner they could lift a man off the floor and up the walls, and then just let him drop. They'd repeat this until their fun was over. Then they beat the man unmercifully, dragged him off the ward, and next morning I learned of his death, the death certificate reading, of course, "Died while being restrained."

Occasionally a doctor (I never did know if he was a psychiatrist) would come through the ward, surrounded by hacks. The patients would all start hollering for him and he would wave them off, and the cops would push them back, and he would disappear off the ward. I never understood the purpose of his coming on the ward, unless it was to sightsee. He certainly never talked to anyone or listened to any of the patients. The ones who decided if you were to be discharged were the hacks. They would recommend your discharge when they got around to it, then you'd appear before a staff, which supposedly consisted of three psychiatrists, and in five minutes it would be determined if you were sane enough to be released. The quickest way to get discharged, though a bit dangerous, was to either escape or try to escape. They figured if you were sane enough to try this you were sane enough to be released. There were many escapes while I was there. On one occasion nine guys went at the same time, in broad daylight. Generally, the bars were sawn with hacksaw blades that were either bought from a guard, or smuggled in on a visit.

My friend Bobby approached me one day and told me he was determined to get out, and that he had already asked his wife to bring up some diamond hacksaw blades. Without even thinking about it, I said count me in. Really, this was foolish of me, because by now, I already had more than half my time in, and had a good thing going at the time. Not being one that looked ahead to the penalties involved in getting caught, but rather craving the excitement involved, I was all for it. We carefully selected two other fellows we knew that we could trust and whom we knew wanted to split because of their charges being heavy.

On his next visit, Bobby got the blades from his wife, and we hid them by taping them to the bottom of an officer's locker. Their lockers were in a room generally kept locked, but many times I had access to the key. We planned and agreed that the best place to saw the bar was in an alcove just off the dormitory. Before going into the dorms at night, all the patients must take their clothes off and leave them on their chairs in the day room. You then have to be in pajamas if you had them or your underwear. This posed the first problem. Once we went into the dorm for the night, there was no way possible to get back out to the day room for our clothes, and we certainly couldn't leave in our underwear. We each had bed slippers so the footwear problem was solved. We only had to walk down the road a short way where his wife would be waiting in a car. We needed shirts and pants, not only because of it being so cold out, but just so that in case someone spotted us walking down the road they wouldn't necessarily know we were escapees. We could be anybody, for all they would know. Sawing the bar wouldn't be much of a problem, because although two officers sat and watched the dorm at night they couldn't see into the alcove, and besides, they generally slept in the corridor between the dorm and day room.

We decided it would take at least three nights to saw through the bars safely. We would then leave just a bit of steel uncut so it wouldn't take more than ten minutes to saw through the night we decided to go. We had the biggest problem in being sure the other patients didn't know, because we would be sure to get ratted on. We took turns in the early morning hours crawling under beds and into the hall that led to the alcove. We had to saw very slow and deliberate to avoid the squeaking noise that accompanies the sawing of bars. And you must also be careful not to let the blade get too hot from the friction, or it snaps very easily. We kept

56

rubbing butter on the blade in hopes of avoiding the blade heating up too much. Each night, before we went back to our beds, we took chewing gum and rolled it in dirt and then stuck it into the groove we had cut. This was to prevent anyone from spotting it as they walked by. The hacks occasionally went on a security check; they were supposed to do it daily, I believe, but they got into the routine of just doing it whenever they felt like. Of course, any check would have uncovered the sawn bar immediately, because the check consisted of running a nightstick across the bars. They have a certain sound when the stick bounces off each intact bar, but when the stick hits a sawn bar, there is a dull thunk, and the sound is obvious. So this was a constant risk, and we therefore couldn't put off going too long.

Soon the bar was sawn just about all the way through, and we faced the problem of getting clothes into the ward. Once we decided the night we were to go I called Bobby's wife. Because of my connections with the gambling ring I didn't have too much trouble using a phone, and in a roundabout way let her know we were going that night, and she should meet us in the prearranged spot. Then came my biggest problem. Because of my being able to maneuver around more freely than the others, I undertook the task of getting the clothes into the dorm. This was the biggest risk, and I delighted in the scheme and thrill of going about it. Four pairs of pants and four shirts made too big a package to carry into the ward, so I had to make two trips which doubled the risk. Finding a place to hide them on the ward posed another problem, since the mattresses were folded back during the day, and hiding places were nonexistent. I planned to put them in a room along the alcove. These rooms were for men who for one reason or another (overcrowdedness or punishment) weren't to sleep in the ward. There were some old fucked-up locks on these doors, with wood chipped away. I went back to the alcove with a pick I fashioned out of a bedspring. Sure enough the lock gave easily, and I knew everything was going to be just great. I picked up extra clothes I had stashed in the broom closet, and waited my chance to hide them in the room.

Everything was all set. I had enough money on me to see me through out of New York. I didn't have any definite plans after I got out; I guess I fantasized a bit imagining I would make some big scores. Beyond that I didn't know what, nor bothered to think about it. I never did give a thought about maybe getting caught on any crime I ever committed. Criminals seldom do. Anyway we were going that night and we could see no hassles. The hard part was over. Or was it? How could we have foreseen the unknown element?

What happened was that at two in the morning as we each took turns sneaking and crawling under beds into the alcove—the hacks completely unaware of anything happening, we were sure to have a couple of hours start before anyone knew of our being missing—a fellow named Carl woke up and looked at the bed next to him in which Freddy slept. Well, Freddy wasn't there, he had already snuck back into the alcove and was waiting for me, all set to go. Carl got shook when he saw the empty bed, because Freddy had been trying to fuck Carl for some time, always hitting on him, and waking him at night by grabbing his ass. So immediately Carl looked around the ward for Freddy. He couldn't find him naturally, so he sat on the edge of his bed looking all around very nervously; he was terrified of Freddy raping him, and I guess he assumed that since Freddy was up, he'd fuck with him if he went back to sleep. I was watching all this, waiting for my chance to slip out of bed and get to the alcove. The time was going and we were already late according to schedule. I kept willing him to lay down, but he seemed scared and kept twitching around. I thought about going

58

over and cold-cocking him, and I would have if I thought he would let me get close to him. Getting to his bed would have meant crossing the middle aisle, and right into the hacks' view if they weren't asleep.

I knew the guys waiting for me were wondering what was going on. I just hoped they didn't panic. One of the hacks started squiriming in his chair. He was waking up, he was getting up. Oh God damn, what fucking shit. I could have killed that punk-kid. I saw Bobby looking at me from the alcove hall. He came to see what was happening. I tried to get the message across to him and pointed at Carl. Bobby immediately picked up what I was telling him. If it wasn't so serious, I would have laughed at the situation. Here was Bobby on the other side of the ward, and me on the opposite with the punk between us, and yet neither of us could get near enough to him to put him out.

A noise turned my head. The hack had gotten up and was looking into the ward at Carl sitting on his bed. With no suspicion, just curiosity, and nothing else to do since he woke up, he sauntered down the aisle towards Carl. I motioned to Bobby to get down—the man was coming—and he ducked out of sight. I could hear Carl and the hack mumbling about something. I prayed it was nothing more than the hack telling him to go to sleep. Everything was so quiet. I lay there not daring to move. The hack turned and slowly walked to the bathroom. I could see he knew nothing of what was going on so far, but when he didn't find Freddy in the bathroom he would damn sure know something was wrong. Suddenly he turned and went over to where his chair was. Whew, a sigh of relief escaped. He was forgetting about it and going back to sit. But no, he had gone over just to pick up his cigarettes, lit one and headed back for the bathroom. While all this was going on Bobby had gotten Freddy and Victor, who were waiting in the alcove. There was nothing they could do. They couldn't finish sawing the bar and split because since the man was in the ward, he'd be sure to hear it. They couldn't get back to their beds past Carl, without him seeing them even if they crawled. I quickly saw the situation, them trying to get back to bed, the man almost to the bathroom now, so I called fairly low to Carl so he would hear me, but not the cop. Carl turned and looked at me and in that instant all three of the guys in the alcove hallway got down and crawled back into the wards and toward their beds. Freddy, being that he slept next to Carl, had the biggest problem. How was he going to get back into bed without Carl seeing him. He couldn't, so while Carl had his attention to me Freddy stood up two beds from him and pretended he was just strolling back to bed after coming from the bathroom. Carl jumped when he heard Freddy behind him, and I could just picture what was going through his head then. He didn't have the slightest idea about any break going on—it didn't even enter his head—but still he knew something was wrong. The hack had just finished looking in the bathroom, and was coming out when he spotted Freddy just getting into bed. I could see the look on his face; he was still very calm about this whole thing, and I am sure he had no suspicions whatever. At the very most, he figured Freddy was probably fucking someone in bed, and had just finished. As I said homosexuality was pretty much allowed. It was no big thing. He continued walking toward Freddy's bed, probably for no other reason than to pass a wisecrack. But Freddy had his clothes on. Carl saw this, but as of yet the hack didn't because Freddy quickly covered himself up with the blanket. I heard him threatening Carl about keeping his mouth shut. Carl's voice raised, and by then the hack was there and asking what was going on. The man could see Carl was really upset about something, so without saying anything to Freddy, he told Carl to come with him. I knew then, the thing was blown.

60

By now many of the men were awake and wondering what was going on. I just hoped Bobby and Victor could get rid of their clothes without any trouble. The man still hadn't gotten out of the ward. He called to the other cop, who had woken up, and told him to keep an eye on Freddy. Anyway Carl blabbed about Freddy having his clothes on, and only then did the significance of the whole thing dawn on the hack. He quickly put the lights on, and not a man could move without being seen clearly by the cops. He dialed a number and in a few minutes a gang of cops came storming on the ward. It was an alarm number that just had to be dialed. The cops swarmed into the ward, and everyone had to get out of bed and stand there by their bed. I was watching Bobby and Victor all the while wondering if they had gotten their clothes off. I saw them get out of bed wearing their shorts only. Whew, what a relief. Meantime the cops grabbed Freddy and hustled him off the ward, while other cops went through the ward tearing beds apart and searching. Just a few beds from Bobby and Victor, I saw the cops pick up shirts and pants. After a lot of questioning no one volunteered where they came from. Obviously Bobby and Victor had kicked them away without anyone seeing them. The place was carefully searched, the bars were checked and ultimately they found the sawn bar, and also the set of clothes in the back that were mine.

We were all forced to go into the day room and sit in our chairs. We all sat up the rest of the night, while they took turns calling guys into different rooms and interrogating them. The questions and punches came in about equal number. By now there were about 30 hacks on the ward, and most of them were just indiscriminately slapping us around, amidst threats of further punishments unless someone came up with the facts. They threatened to turn the ward into a jail ward where we would have to spend the whole day sitting in our chairs without any privileges such as smoking or reading and T.V. I wasn't concerned with these broad threats. In fact I would have gladly settled for that. My fear was that someone saw Bobby and Victor getting rid of their clothes, and that guy would either tell out of fear or just to get in favor with the cops. I wasn't too much worried about myself. I was sure that none of the guys would rat on me.

Eventually I was called in to the room and asked what did I know. I told them the whole thing was a surprise to me. Of course they didn't believe me. They insisted that I knew of everything that went on in the ward and most of the joint. They said unless I opened up I would be shipped to the Jail Ward, and I knew what goes on there. They started pushing me around, and getting rough. My attitude didn't help me much, either. This infuriated them. They ultimately let me go out to the day room and resume sitting and waiting. Soon the night hack that had been talking with Carl came from the back, said a few words to the other cops and they called me back into the room. They insisted I was in on it; they knew all about it, they claimed. Carl saw the whole thing, and Freddy told them I was in on it. Of course I knew they were just fishing and I kept denying it. Eventually it boiled down to me being awake and up talking to Carl when the shit was going on. This convinced them I was part of the escape. By now they had found out from someone that Bobby and Victor had thrown the clothes on the floor. They were taken to the back rooms along with Freddy.

Later that day Bobby and Victor were transferred to another ward, and in about a week they were discharged. I later found out they had not been beaten too bad. Certainly not the way Freddy was. When they took me into the back rooms I had to go past the room where they were beating him. He was on the floor, bloody, and between kicks and calling him nigger, they were beating him with their keys.

62

These keys are large skeleton keys about six on a chain, attached to a long chain anchored to their belts. To be beaten with these was terribly painful. There was actually shit all over him and the floor. He had literally and figuratively had the shit beaten out of him. His moans were terrible to the ears, and it was a terrible sight to see. The reasons I can assume he was beaten so badly were because he was black, because he never got a visit so they had no reason for worrying about anyone seeing him in that condition, and because he was the only one actually caught in the act. I was forced to strip, slapped around some but only halfheartedly because some of the hacks in the group were deeply involved with Mendy. My clothes were taken and I was left in the room naked. Ironically, this was the same room that I had opened the lock to hide all the clothes in, and it was right next to the window that the bar was sawn out of.

I stayed in the room for several days; the hacks let Jimmy give me food and cigarettes, or rather some of them did. Freddy was sent to the jail ward and I never heard about him again. By the time I was let out of the room, Bobby and Victor were sent back to court to face their original charges. For a while security was tighter, but that didn't last long. I was let out of the room in about two weeks, I think. When my clothes were returned, naturally the few hundred dollars I had in them was gone. I didn't bother to bitch about it; it wouldn't have done any good. I was transferred to another ward, and I was never able to get back into any action. Jimmy took good care of me, though, so I never really needed anything.

I was getting bored with the place now, and each day was a drag. I signed up with the softball team and that was a gas. No ball game could ever be compared to these games, and a lot of money would be bet on them. A typical game went like this: First, the ball field was small and a decent clout of the ball would hit the back wall, and if it was caught on the fly, the rebound off the wall, it was an out. If it went on the roof it was a homer. You could hit a solid low line drive, and it would bounce off the wall so hard, you'd be lucky not to get thrown out at first base. One old black fellow, I remember, was a damned good hitter, but dig, on the way around the bases he would stop and do somersaults. It was hilarious, especially on the way to first base. You see, the batter was not allowed to drop the bat at home plate, for fear some nut would pick it up and go berserk. And so after your turn at bat you had to either hand it to the batter behind you or run down to first base and drop it there where a cop was standing. So picture this guy hitting the ball, doing flips on the way to first with a bat in his hand. But he was needed on the team because first of all there weren't that many sane people that liked to play softball under those conditions, and besides he was a good hitter. The best pitcher was shell-shocked. From what I had heard, he was once in the navy and his ship was bombed and sunk and he was one of the few survivors. Well he was one hell of a pitcher, but his hangup was that if any plane came overhead, he would run like hell to the bathroom and hide under one of the toilets. So naturally our games were held up several times.

Soon after came the incident that caused my being discharged and sent back to Coxsackie. On the grounds in a separate building was a complex of living quarters for hacks that didn't live in town. Their rooms were cleaned by some of the patient trusties. One day Mike, a fellow I knew not too well, came over to rap with me. It seems he had stolen $500 from one of the cop's rooms and he had no way to get rid of it or use it. He wasn't too well in the head, and he couldn't approach a cop to buy things for him. He was there several years and never received money from anyone. So he had this bread and didn't know what to do with it. What he had in mind was that when I got a visit I could give the money,

64

minus my end to my visit and they would then send it to him under a different name.

I told him okay; I didn't really give much thought, as I never did, to the penalties of getting involved. He said he hid the money in a bed post in the ward. I told him that wasn't too cool because that was generally one of the first places they looked when there was a big shakedown. I anticipated a hell of a search when the cop realized he was missing the dough. So the stupid bastard goes back to the ward to get the money right when everyone is in the day room. Alan, a real creep, obviously spots that he is up to something and follows him into the ward and sees him get the money. Alan's the type of person that thrives on bullying others weaker than himself, and he has no heart or balls himself. He wasn't too well liked by many. Alan demands to be cut in or else he would beat the shit out of Mike, and he threatened to tell the man. Mike went along with it, out of fear, plus he had no thought in his mind other than having some money; $100 or $200 was all the same to him. He had been without money for so long $100 was a great deal of money to him. He comes back to me and tells me what happened and about Alan. I ask him if he told Alan about me being in on it and he swears he didn't. I kind of believe it because I feel that if Alan did know I was in on it he wouldn't have threatened the kid. Alan was pretty much afraid of me. Mike tells me he hid the money, along with Alan, behind a radiator. This pisses me off; they don't have the brains of an asshole. I'm afraid also that the punk Alan is going to rip the money off and then swear he knows nothing about it.

I make up my mind to get the bread and stash it myself without either of them knowing. A good friend of mine was getting a visit that weekend and he takes care of the business for me. It was just a few days away and the money had to get off the ward quick. I told Mike to leave the money where he put it, everything was all right, and I would get it when I got my visit. He had no suspicions whatsoever. I waited my chance, snuck into the ward, and got the money, and had to hide under a bed to avoid getting busted by a cop making the rounds of the dorm.

While hiding under the bed, I started getting the feeling this whole thing was getting to be too hassled. I got bad vibes from it, and I kind of felt I was going to get jammed. But as I so often did, I ignored the feelings and planned to go through with it. I hadn't yet decided whether to keep the whole thing or to give Mike a hundred dollars and keep the rest. I taped the money to the bottom of the hacks' locker. It was the one place they never thought of looking when they frisked the place.

Mike went back out to work next morning, and I felt uneasy the whole time. Sure enough, I was called to the office; the hacks there didn't even know what I was wanted for, but they wanted me downstairs. Without a doubt, I knew what it was all about. An army of cops seemed to be there, and as I passed the room next to the one I had to go to, I heard them beating someone. Naturally it was Mike. The cops started questioning me and they were really angered. I knew this was a bad situation, but so far, they didn't know I was involved. Mike hadn't told them a thing. I found this out by the way they questioned me. Only because of my reputation, and being the biggest schemer on the ward, they figured I had to be in on it. There were only a few sane guys on the whole ward, and they didn't figure to get involved in something like this.

The cops told me I better get the money up, or else they wouldn't play any games this time when it came to working me over. They assured me they would find out all about it if they had to kill Mike. Some of the cops seemed insane in their anger and I did get shook up. I kept denying it, there

66

wasn't anything else I could do. They belted me around, and while it was a pretty bad beating I felt it was only the beginning. They brought me up to the ward, and locked me in a room. Then about twenty of them turned the ward upside down. Everyone was stripped and searched thoroughly. The cops told them if anyone knew about what happened to the money they better talk now, or else the whole ward was going to be worked over. Most of these guys were so out of it, they couldn't even absorb what the cops were talking about.

I was locked in the room all day, and could hear them continuing throughout the day, tearing things up, and questioning people. They didn't bother me anymore, and this kind of scared me. Jimmy hadn't come at food time, so obviously they wouldn't let him. About eight or nine at night, some charge came in my room, and talked very levelly with me, saying they were determined to get the money back, and they would, and my only chance was to talk now and save myself a lot of aggravation if they found out I was involved. I claimed I was getting a bad deal just cause some hacks didn't like me, and I knew nothing. I insisted I seldom if ever even talked with Mike, cause he wasn't in my class. He walked out saying it was up to me. I lay down and just prayed I got through this, saying I wouldn't fuck around again. This was bullshit, cause I always said that. It was kind of like a deal I'd make with some unknown power, but neither he nor I ever kept our words.

The next day things were quiet, too quiet. Then the silence was broken by the sounds of the cops coming with determined steps. This was it. I knew they knew. Without stopping for one minute to say anything but curses at me, they started working me over. And it was bad, believe me. They all pummeled me some with blackjacks, and some with fists. It seemed like every blow caused some light flashing in

67

my head. I had absolutely no chance to put up a fight, even if I intended or wanted to. I was knocked to the ground and kicked repeatedly. The hacks were getting in each other's way in their attempts to get at me. I heard some say to the others, "Step back, let me at him." I kept cursing and hollering at them and this only made them worse. But I just couldn't let them beat me without fighting back in some way. I have no idea how long it lasted, my body hurt in so many places, it was just one dull pain. There was blood all over my body, and a few even gave me some final kicks because I had got blood on them. They left and I couldn't move. I just lay there feeling so fucked up. I didn't know if I would live or die, and I don't think I cared.

I lay there several hours I guess, or so it seemed. I made an attempt to get up, but none of my muscles would support me. Finally an inmate nurse was let into my room, cleaned up only the worst gashes and squeezed my bones to see if any were broken. In about five minutes he left, just as cold as he came in. Then some guards came in with a restraining sheet, lifted and threw me on the bed and tied me to the bed with the canvas sheet. They forced my limbs into position, and the pain was excruciating. When they got through, I could move only my head a few inches from side to side. Then the inmate nurse came back in and forced salts down my throat. I could only lay there, completely helpless, not able to move any part of my painful body. My body screamed to be moved into a less painful position. I had to get out; I really didn't believe I could endure this for even five minutes more. But I did. I had to. The body can absorb an incredible amount of punishment when it has to. I didn't think I would ever be whole again. I began to think about what a fucked up life I had. And all I really ever wanted was a chance, a break, someone to help me get straight. It's all I ever wanted.

I remained that way all night; naturally I couldn't sleep.

68

I think it was the longest night of my life, up till then. Since then, I've experienced other such nights. Sometime next morning, I was given some powdered milk to drink. Generally I hated the stuff, and never drank it, but that morning, my need for something to drink, caused me to want more. Naturally they wouldn't give me more. I kept thinking they had to let me out if only to let a doctor see me. I kept waiting for footsteps in the hall, but none came. And then I felt the desperate need to move my bowels. I tightened my muscles to hold it in. My belly started hurting from the need to shit. Suddenly it just came out, a stinking gooey shit that just ran out over my legs and ass. God, it was terrible. A feeling of filth and disgust filled me. And I had to continue laying there. The stench became horrible, I started gagging, and watery vomit flowed from my mouth. Because I couldn't move my head enough, the vomit ran down my cheek, and on my neck. They had to let me out. They couldn't let me lay like this. But they did. No one cared.

I stayed like that all day and early in the evening when the night shift came on, one of the bastards came in and forced more salts down my throat. I was given some more powdered milk to drink. I dozed off and on during the night, and it seemed like a nightmare I couldn't wake from. In the morning, they came back in and asked where the money was. I insisted I didn't know. Then they told me they had given Mike sodium pentothal and he admitted I was in on it. I swore I had no idea where the money was. Can you picture being strapped down, completely helpless, with shit and vomit all over, and being interrogated and threatened by a bunch of sadistic goons surrounding your bed? It's not a good position, and one of complete humiliation. I couldn't afford to admit being part of the scheme, even if I wanted to, which I didn't. It seems Mike had told them where he had last hidden the money, but they couldn't find it there naturally.

69

Just while they were questioning me more shit ran out of my ass. The room was already smelling so bad, from the past days, that the hacks had opened the window and they moved to the window inhaling fresh air. I was inured to the stink by now. After threatening me some more, I guess they saw I was not going to say anything further, and they couldn't be sure someone else had found the money and kept it. Even some hack while they were searching for it, may have found it and said nothing. I had half convinced them I really didn't know any more about it. I remained that night tied down, and next day they released me.

When they removed the sheet from my body, I looked down at my body, and the sight was a disgusting one. It was one mass of swellings, black and blue marks, crusted blood and shit stuck to my thighs and legs. It seemed like a cloud of stink arose from my body as soon as the sheet was off. The inmate that untied me, was gagging all the while, and several times he had to run to the window to inhale fresh air. I remember the first motion I made to rise. The aches and pain ran through the entire length of my body. No muscle would react to my wish to move. Each of my joints seemed to be welded together. God, it was awful. I couldn't do more than roll a bit on my back from side to side. The cold air caused the raw spots on my body, which were from the rubbing of the canvas sheet, a great deal of pain. The thought flashed through my mind that I wouldn't ever really recover from this. I was going to be crippled in some way because of this. I was scared to death. They told me to get up and get to the shower. Believe me, I wanted to, but I couldn't move. The pain was unbearable. I lay there and slowly forced my knees to flex, despite the pain. The other inmate went and got a wheelchair for me, and slowly we got me into it. He then wheeled me into the shower, and I stayed in the chair while the warm water ran on me. Needless to say, it took some time for me to get my movements coordinated.

I was kept locked in the room for about ten days. Depending on the hack, Jimmy would bring me candy, cigarettes and good meals. I was able to tell him where the money was hid. We agreed it was best to leave it there till I got out of the room, and things quieted down. I learned Mike was transferred to the jail ward. God help him. Jimmy told me there was a rumor going around that I was to be transferred back to Coxsackie. I was glad of that because I knew I wasn't going to be treated too well if I remained in this place. Sure enough, a few days later, I was brought down to staff, the three psychiatrists who would decide about me in a matter of minutes. They asked me a few stupid questions, and whether I felt better now than when I came in. They then told me they felt I had responded to treatment (?) and that I was well now. All this without ever receiving any medication, therapy, or any guidance or discussions at all.

I was to be shipped out within the next few days. Jimmy said he'd try to maneuver so he could get to my room for a few hours, so we could say our farewells in bed. I was terribly infatuated with Jimmy and I made up my mind to meet with him on the streets. The next evening when the night shift came on (four to midnight) Jimmy was able to come in my room until shortly before lights out at ten. It was truly a remarkable experience. Jimmy was as much as a woman could be.

I was returned to Coxsackie but this time there was a big difference. I now had a reputation. I wasn't someone to be fucked with. I spent most of my remaining time in segregation. I had learned a few of the state rules while in Matteawan and one of them was that a person in a reformatory wasn't to be deprived of a chance at education. So when the

71

P.K. sentenced me to segregation this time I insisted on being allowed school books. His reaction to this wasn't too good but I insisted I knew by state rules I was allowed to have them. After a lot of bullshit, some books were brought to my cell. I read every minute of the day. Mostly ancient history. The time passed much more quickly.

Even finishing up my three-year sentence in segregation wasn't enough for the P.K. When I had eleven days to go before they had to discharge me, he put me in strip cell for the remaining ten days, saying he was giving me a chance to meditate on my life. That motherfucker. I did the ten days hating a bit more each day. All I could think of was getting even. I hated him, his mother, every hack, every person in society. Somehow I would get even. I thought of a million ways of torturing him. I fantasized about some way of blowing the whole fucking place up. I paced up and down like a caged tiger every waking moment of those ten days. I couldn't wait to get out. I'd get a gun and come up and kill this motherfucker. Someone was going to pay for what happened to me. People were going to know I was alive, I was a person, I existed.

7

During the train ride home I tried to think of where I was at. What was I going to do? I was nothing more than a young kid, without the wherewithal to construct my life into anything meaningful. I was angry at so much, with many people. And yet where do I put the blame? With the exception of a certain few whom I knew I hated, who were the rest I hated? The nameless society. They were responsible for allowing these things happen to me, but just who is the nameless society? I was so confused in my thoughts. All I knew was that I didn't want to be a part of such a rotten group of people. I was going to be accepted in their world but only as a subhuman. Well, fuck them. I didn't want to be a part of them. They didn't want me and I didn't want them.

Walking to my house from the subway I saw the bastard that ratted on me. He stopped when he saw me. I started walking towards him, not knowing what I was going to do, but he quickly ran down a cellar. I wasn't that angry with him. Strange, I should be, but I wasn't. Yet, I would have beat the shit out of him if I caught him. My mother put her arms around me at the door and I realized then, I couldn't stand her. I felt strange looking at my parents. I didn't really feel a part of them. Already they started telling me how I had to be a good boy now, and not get into any more trouble.

I was soon back to hanging out on the streets. There was a gang that hung out at a poolroom two blocks away. When they learned I had just got out of jail after doing three years I was quickly accepted. We fought other gangs, fucked around and stole when we could. Petty stealing. They drank a lot and smoked grass. I didn't drink at all, but I smoked a lot of grass. I felt a little wiser than they. They were still living their youth. I had outlived whatever youth I had.

I became a feared gang member. I had learned in jail to fight dirtier than the next guy. And I had a lot of fight in me. All my anger came out in fighting. Plus I wanted to be the best. I wanted to be the one everyone looked up to. I became known as a good knife fighter. It wasn't that I wanted to hurt the other person, I seldom cut them more than superficially. I just wanted to show I had the biggest balls.

It was then I tried my first shot of heroin. I used to kid the addicts I knew that it was all in their heads, that they didn't really get high. One night we went up to my house and they all shot some heroin. This one guy was too stoned to hit my vein, so I shot it up myself. I didn't feel a damn thing and I had taken as much as they. I laughed at them saying I told you it's all in your head. We sat around for a while and before we left, I decided to shoot up the stuff that was left. I cooked it up and shot it in my vein. No sooner did I get it in when, bang, I felt an enormous rush overpowering me. The next thing I knew I was waking up sick with vomit all over me and it was daylight out. After I cleaned up I went to find out what happened. I learned I had overdosed and they tried to get me out of it and couldn't so they left. This was a very common thing. Your best friends would just leave you there if you

74

O.D.'ed rather than chance getting involved with the cops. If you had money in your pocket they would take that too. I know of times where they took the guy's shoes or jacket if they were nice. After all, a corpse has no use for them.

I tried heroin a couple of times after that, but rather than getting high, all I did was get sick, so I gave it up. Except for some petty stealing I wasn't doing anything. Then one night, we were all at a party. I began drinking and got stoned out of my mind. The brother of the guy that had ratted on me had a car downstairs. I got in it and had a lot of trouble driving it. This was my first time drunk, excepting once when I was about eleven years old, and I drove all over the streets. Eventually the cops pulled me over and the windup was the car was a stolen car. It had been stolen a month before and I got the rap for stealing it. Christ, back in jail. What a fucking drag. About a week later I got out on bail.

I knew I had to get some money for a lawyer so I looked up a friend I met in the county jail and borrowed a gun from him. There was a liquor store just two blocks from where we hung out. It was a prosperous store and he also cashed checks on Friday. I hid a jacket in the hallway across the street and then went into the store. It was easy; I locked him in the back, and took all the bread. I had combed my hair different and tried to talk with a Spanish accent. I left the store, put on the jacket, and went through the back alleys and into a restaurant where two cops were playing pinochle with the owner. About twenty minutes later I went back to the store. There was a big crowd around with plenty of cops, and there was the owner hollering some spic had stuck him up. I knew I had got away clean with about eleven hundred bucks. This was big money to me. Equally important was the exhilarating feeling it gave me. It was a real kick.

I began sticking up liquor stores regular. Then I remembered a five-and-ten store uptown where I had been caught

75

for shoplifting when I was a kid. They had brought me to a room upstairs while waiting for the cops and in the room was a safe. It was where they brought the larger bills and supplied the cash registers downstairs. It looked real easy. So I took it off with a friend of mine.

I bought myself a good secondhand Buick Roadmaster convertible. I drove around feeling no one was better than I. I was running numbers for this bookie but it was a real drag. Very dull and I couldn't stand having to make the commitments to be at a certain place at a certain time. One day this cat down a few blocks had hit the number for two grand. I knew Charlie the guy I worked for would be walking down there to pay the guy. There was a large concrete abutment sticking out over the sidewalk supporting the overpass and I hid behind there in broad daylight. Sure enough here comes Charlie. When he got past me, I hit him with the blackjack. I took the roll of dough and split. That night I get word Charlie wants to see me. I also find out he doesn't have the slightest idea who did it. I see Charlie and he tells me he will give me $500 to get the guy that did it. He gives me $250 up front and the rest after I catch the guy. Needless to say I never did catch the guy.

I was going real crazy. I never stayed still for a minute. It was like an obsession to keep going. Everyone in the neighborhood thought I was crazy. I would do anything, and wasn't afraid of no one. I was still very small and looked like a young kid. The two local beat cops hated me and told me they better not see me in the streets. My car wasn't registered legit, nor did I have a driver's license so I couldn't bring it around the block too tough.

There was this one Irish detective from the next precinct who hated me, along with everyone else, with a passion. I had been picked up in his precinct a few times for suspicion, and there was nothing he loved to do more than beat the shit out of people. He was constantly drunk and this kept him from going higher in the ranks. He had several citations to his credit and he had killed several suspects. On one occasion he was in the back of a liquor store getting drunk, when a guy comes in to rob it. Without any kind of a chance at all, this cop points his gun through the curtain and kills the bandit. Then he runs outside, where the guy had a girl laying chickie. When she heard the shots she started running, and the cop starts shooting at her. Fortunately, he was stoned and she got away. Another time two bandits were backing out of a liquor store they had just stuck up with a knife. This Irish bastard, we'll call him O'Hare, is passing by in an unmarked car. He pulls right up and shoots them both in the back.

He almost had me good one time. I was walking with a friend of mine and we spot O'Hare just as he spots us. I had a gun on me so we started running into this apartment building. We go up to the roof with the cops right behind us. The landing door is locked and there is no way out. I can't get rid of the gun, not even a window to throw it out of. I see a sled leaning up against the wall and there are some newspapers on the floor. I put the gun under the newspapers and lean the sled against the wall with the bottom of the sled on the newspapers. We start going back downstairs to brazen it out. I feel a bullet in my pocket. I drop it on the floor. The cops grab us and bring us downstairs. They search the stairways and find only the bullet. O'Hare starts yelling where's the gun. They bring us to the precinct and I am sure they are going to find the gun. They had searched the hall twice already. O'Hare sends two cops over with a big flashlight to search again. I'm scared to death. Meantime he starts working over my friend. From the next room I can hear him punching my friend. I just hope he has sense enough to keep quiet. Surprisingly, I don't get hit at all. The cops come back and say they could find nothing. I don't believe it. He keeps us there a couple of hours and then warns me he better not ever see me in his precinct again. We get cut loose. I keep looking back sure that we are being followed, but we're not. Hours later, I carefully go back and sure enough the gun is right where I put it. I get the gun and split.

About two weeks later, I am ripping off a loft filled with suits and overcoats. I'm throwing them out the window to a friend who's loading the car with them. Just as we are ready to pull out who gets into the car with us but O'Hare. Oh Christ! Right away all I see is jail. He tells us to drive down the street. He is stone drunk as usual. After threatening us over and over he says he hopes we have some money to take care of this matter. What a break. I had about $400 and my friend $200. We give it to him, and as he is getting out of the car, again he tells me he better never see me in the neighborhood again. This cop is insane.

I was now out on three bails. I had got busted doing a friend a favor. He wanted me to bring some heroin uptown. Instead of going right uptown, I stopped in my neighborhood. That particular night there were a gang of cops stopping and searching everyone and I got busted. I was also out on bail for possession of a pistol. Things were getting touchy in court, to say the least, but I never really gave it too much thought.

Then came a close one. One night I saw cops outside the bar. I knew they would search me when I came out, so I gave my gun to a friend and left. Sure enough they stopped me, and not finding anything they let me go. About a week later O'Hare calls me up and says he wants to talk with me. He says I'm not in any trouble, he just wants to talk with me. I go figuring if I don't he will come after me. I can't think of anything he could get me for. When I get there, a bunch of cops whom I find out are from homicide are there. They start questioning me, not giving me any hint of what it is all about.

They bring me down to O'Hare's office. I see my friend's mother sitting there. Pretty soon they drag my friend out of the room, a bloody mess. She takes one look at her son and faints.

They bring me in next and O'Hare tells the others he'll take care of me. Bam!—he starts slugging me. As usual he is drunk but now he's almost crazy. He is really punching me. He tells me to take my shoes off. When I do, he starts stepping on my toes. He is like an insane man. My face is all bloody and I'm sure he broke my nose. In desperation, I swing back figuring I can't take much more of this. He knocks me down and as I am getting up he kicks my head against the wall. I feel the blood spurting out. Finally one of the homicide cops tells him to leave me alone. He tells the cop he will do what he wants in his precinct. The homicide cop tells him if he wants to keep this precinct he better not hit me again. They bring me down to the bathroom and clean me off.

I'm still asking what this is all about when they bring me up to a station house way uptown. They leave me alone in an office while they question my friend. There is a report on the desk. I sneak a look at it. It's a report on a murder just committed. Oh shit, what a relief. I know damn well I didn't kill anyone. Finally they come in and tell me they got me on a murder charge. I laughed at them, with a sense of relief, and the bastard threw a big glass ash tray and hit me in the head with it. Then they start asking me about the gun I gave to a friend in the bar that night. How the fuck do they know about that? Then I find that the couple hadn't been shot. I feel a lot better, since I can prove where I was on that specific night. They kept me there almost all night; then they bring me to my local precinct, where after a lot of bullshit they let me go.

My next trouble comes up from being a good samaritan. I was walking up the street after the bar closed and I see three men pushing a woman around and she is yelling. I figure they are trying to rape her so I go in and ask her what is the trouble. One of the men runs. She tells me one of the men is her husband and just at that moment he punches me right in the face. I start fighting with both of them. Only because they were drunker than I did I have any chance. I knock him down and as I turn to leave I notice one of my cuff links on the floor. I bend to pick it up and the fuck sticks his finger right in my eye. Furious, I started kicking him in the head. Then I leave. I'm blind in my eye so I go to the emergency room. I spot the broad there and when she sees me she starts talking to a cop. I gave a knife I had to my friend who came to the hospital with me and she sees this. The cop comes over and tells me I am the one that stabbed her husband. She is crazy I say. Anyway I get booked for assault with a deadly weapon; when I kicked him I had cut his head open.

So I am back in jail and I am supposed to be in court on another charge tomorrow. As soon as I get arraigned in court on the assault, I tell my bondsman I got no money on me but I'll bring it later. He has to get me out so I can get over to felony court or else the judge there will revoke my bail. He bails me out and I barely get to court on time. This broad had to be crazy. I don't know what's in her mind. She knows I was trying to help her. When I go to court on that case I tell the husband that I will pay him if the case is dropped. He is sympathetic about the whole thing but it seems his wife is running the show. She sees me talking to him and yells in the courtroom I am threatening him. I never did figure that whole thing out.

That's the last time I'll ever help anybody again, I tell myself.

Just about this time, heroin was really spreading out in the neighborhoods. Most of my friends were on it. It was good stuff then and cheap; when you got strung out you were really strung out. In the later years and the present days, if a junkie got busted he would hardly even be sick and he would be eating the first meal that came around. I remember those times when I was in jail. A guy would come in strung out. He would be laying on the floor for about two or three days with stomach cramps and vomiting. He wouldn't be able to eat for three days, and you didn't get any sympathy from the cops in the jail.

There was a narcotics squad formed. About five cops I believe and one was a broad. This broad was too much. She would shack up with a guy if she thought he was a pusher. She would be his old lady until she could set him up for a bust. One of the cops, now pretty famous, was a bitch. He was a rough bastard. He would stop you anywhere and search you and push you around whether or not you had drugs on you. He was well known to put drugs in your pocket and say he busted you with a stash. He would bust a guy with drugs, turn in half the stuff, and give the other half to a junkie to push for him. Then he would bust the guys that copped from this junkie. He would take your money and tell you if you said anything about it he would shoot you, or he'd tell you he would set you up for a big bust. Everybody was in it for the money. There was a lot to be made from it. Without the help of the cops, I personally doubt that drugs would be as prevalent today as they are.

I remember one time running from some cops. I run up to a friend's house and who do you think is there stone naked. This lady narco cop. I try to catch my friend alone in the kitchen to pull his coat, but she suspects something and won't leave the room. It sure was a funny feeling. Here I am with the cops after me, and right in front of me is a naked lady cop. A couple hours later I split and call my friend up. When I tell

81

him he doesn't believe me. Finally I convince him. Next thing I heard he had split the apartment and didn't come back.

I got my first serious gunshot just about then. I had been shot twice in the shin while gunfighting with a .22. This time I was running from the cops and as I was going over a fence one of the cops hit me in the back of the thigh with a .38 bullet. Christ, it hurt. The cops couldn't climb the fence evidently cause I heard them hollering on the other side. I got myself to a friend's house, and he called the bookie I used to work for. He sent a doctor over to take the bullet out. When he saw I was just a kid—I still looked very young—he was afraid, and said he couldn't come any more. My fucking leg was killing me, but eventually it healed.

While laid up with my leg, it was the first time I stopped to think of what I had been doing. It came to me that this wasn't really what I wanted to be doing. I asked myself why I was doing it then, and I just couldn't answer it. I felt there was no other world for me, and in order to survive I had to live in this type of world. I wished I could just wipe it all away, the things I had done, the cases in court, and be like any other kid and live a normal life. But I knew I wasn't like any other kid. Something inside was driving me.

I decided to try to go straight when my leg healed up. I got a job in a bakery working nights. I was going to court pretty regularly now on all my cases. I knew I was a damn fool for working for peanuts when the only way I could beat these cases was to steal enough money to buy a break in court. But I kept working. After two weeks, I cut my hand very badly. The butcher doctor in the emergency room barely cleaned the grease from around the cuts he stitched. Like a fool, out of habit, I had given a false name at the hospital. This, I was later told, prevented me from suing the bakery for a lot of money. When they took the stitches out, pus was oozing out. The doctor did a half-assed job of dressing it and told me to soak it. I just let it go.

Pretty soon my fingers and hand were swollen grotesquely. I still didn't pay it too much mind. A girl I dated made me go to her doctor. He was ready to cut it open and I got up and walked out. He warned me I might lose my hand, but didn't pay him any mind. Finally, I slept home one night. I had been walking around kind of feverish and was too tired to go to my place. My father saw my hand in the morning and made me go with him to New York Hospital. There they immediately checked me in and at first they felt they would have to amputate. They decided a couple days more wouldn't matter too much, and they would see if I responded to treatment for those few days.

Fortunately I did. The seriousness of the whole thing just didn't dawn on me. Looking back on my life now it is obvious I was totally self-destructive to a dangerous degree.

Finally they revoked my bail. The gun charge and the drug case couldn't be tried for lack of evidence. It is ironic because they were the two I was guilty of. They prosecuted me on the stolen car and the assault case. Both of these I was innocent of.

I didn't know the first thing about law. No one did then among the inmates. It wasn't like it is today where the first thing everybody does when he gets busted is to read a lawbook or talk over his case with a jailhouse lawyer. They didn't even let you have a lawbook years ago. My lawyer, the shyster bastard, convinced me to plead guilty to Grand Larceny and I would get at the most three years. I tried to explain that I didn't steal the car, but he said don't worry, he had talked it over with the judge and I'll only get the three years.

I was later to find out he was one of the biggest thieves I ever met. He would get all these cases, especially from the Spanish people who couldn't speak English, get whatever money he could from them and then talk them into pleading guilty. He has caused hundreds of people to spend many more years in prison than they should have. With another lawyer, most likely they would have received half the sentence they did with him. A real unscrupulous sell-out bastard.

I went to court for sentence. My girl was in court and when she heard the judge say five to ten years at hard labor she fainted. I didn't feel too good either. I was shocked. To appease me the lawyer quickly told me he was going to appeal, which was a crock of shit. I walked out of the courtroom real cocky flipping a coin. I didn't want anyone to see how I felt inside. A few minutes later the lawyer comes to the bullpen and has the balls to ask for the rest of the money. I reached through the bars and if I could have grabbed him I would have strangled the motherfucker.

The full import of the term doesn't hit you till days later. The judge said I was to receive psychiatric treatment and if I behaved myself I would be home in three years. I remembered the last judge that told me some bullshit too. I wasn't yet twenty-one and here I was going to state prison for ten years. God, what a heartless bastard you must be.

I walked through the doors of the state prison. There were eleven of us new "Mickeys." A real hillbilly-looking guard lined us up; he had this three-foot-long club in his hand. I remember the first thing he told us. "You city slickers listen up. They had to run me down to put shoes on me, by God, but I'm your boss." For emphasis he banged the club on the floor. I'll tell you, I was pretty scared. When they marched us through one area of the prison to get a uniform and stuff, I could see the other inmates sizing me up. I was still damn small and hadn't yet started to shave. Shit, I don't want to have to go through that again, I thought.

While being taken to the cell assigned to each of us, there was a rumpus in the block. A big black guy with a butcher knife in his hand was chasing another inmate. I saw him catch up to the guy at the end of the block and cold bloodedly stick the knife right in his stomach. It took a few moments for it to dawn on me that he was killing the other guy deliberately. Guards came running out of nowhere. Bells were ringing, voices were yelling. They slammed us in cells. Pretty soon everything had died down but the buzzing of the inmates. I was to find out that the guy that did the stabbing was a homosexual. Wow, not exactly what I would expect from a fag. I was still a very naive person. Soon I would find out some of the toughest men in prison were homosexuals.

Laying in my cell, I heard canaries singing, men talking and saw inmates walking all around the cells. This really seemed strange because in the reformatory no inmate walked around like that. There was much less regimentation in state prison. In this particular prison, I found out, the inmates were allowed to do their own thing to a great extent.

8

The train ride to the city was a long one. This was a milk train and it stopped constantly. I settled back in the seat and watched the countryside roll by. I was free, finally. Six long years. Six years of hell, of being treated as subhuman, of constant harassment and punishment. All in the name of our great society.

I wondered just how many people could survive what some of us had to go through. I wondered just how many people would even believe the things we lived through in prison. I thought of the atrocities that prisoner of war captives endure. Yet it isn't quite the same. They went over there to deliberately kill. And they did it with a purpose, whether it be for patriotic reasons or what. They believed they had something to fight for; they had a cause, for God and America or something like that. When you have a cause or a belief you can accept things far better. But we in prison had no beliefs, no causes, and nothing really to fight for except our own sanity. Most prisoners of war either killed the enemy or participated in the killing of the enemy. But the majority of men in prison never killed nor even physically hurt any-one.

When you see the guards ganging up and beating another inmate senselessly, and you know you're not even capable of doing such an act (yet you're called the animal, not the guards) it's hard for you to accept society's justice. When you are in prison for stealing a car, and you commit a minor infraction and they place you in solitary, man there's just no way you can say to yourself, "I did something wrong, and I am being punished fairly." When you see guards that are supposed to be the representatives of society's just and fair men act lower than you would ever dream of, it's impossible not to become bitter. I didn't want to be a part of that hypo-critical society. They were more callous than I ever could be. And since there is no middle line, I went to the other side.

I thought of these things while going home. I thought of all that I learned in my past life. I could see no place that I fit in. What was there for me to believe in? Certainly not justice. Oh no! I had seen justice at work. Justice wasn't blind. It could see well enough to determine that if you had money you either got off or got a light sentence. And if you had no money you got a longer prison term. And if you had no money in prison, many many nights you went to bed hungry, and no one gave a fuck. To survive in prison you have to learn to hustle, to con, to steal, to be violent.

The prison system is set up in a manner that you learn these things naturally. You learn to be indifferent when you see another being beaten viciously or harassed by the guards. You push your feelings down deep inside you, where it will take years for them ever to surface again. I couldn't do this. I couldn't swallow my sensitivity. I felt it whenever another person suffered. I couldn't accept the philosophy, "Well, that's the way it goes." If you were going to punish me in the name of justice, well then God damn it, give me justice.

Don't be a hypocrite about it. And God damn it, don't expect me to react towards it nicely and respect you for it.

I have never been a meek follower, a conformer. I am an aggressive person and when I don't like what's happening I am going to speak up. This attitude made me stand out in prison. Just about every guard knew me and disliked me. Some men can go to prison and hardly anyone notices they're even there. They abide by all the rules, accept whatever is being done to them, and sort of get lost in the crowd. I happen not to be one of those. I may not be able to win, but I'm damn sure not going to die quietly. You're going to know I existed.

Somewhere during those six years, I decided it was me against them. And my ego demanded I wasn't going to become a robot, a broken man. And it was my ego that gave me the strength to survive some hellish tortures. I didn't particularly care about living. If I died, I died, and life hadn't shown me anything so great that I should treasure living.

I thought back to when I was fourteen years old. I was before a judge in children's court. My charge was nothing more than malicious mischief, yet the judge had predicted that if I didn't change my attitude I would die in the streets shot by a cop or else die in the electric chair. What a hell of a thing to tell a fourteen-year-old. Do we give up on our children so easily?

What had I learned during the last six years? I learned how to break rock with a sledgehammer. I learned how to mop floors, but then I had a lot of experience doing that in other places. Six years out of your life and not one good memory. On the contrary, my memory was full of hate, disgust, pain, and confusion.

I thought of all the poor people being fucked by this great society. Paying more than their share of taxes compared to the rich men, breaking their asses all their lives to survive, while the leaders of the country manipulate their way to wealth through fraud, deceit and downright stealing. And the little people aren't even aware of what's happening, or if some are, they just accept it resignedly. I thought of all the hungry children in America while the rich throw parties that cost 50 grand or more. I thought of all the damn fools that went overseas to fight wars motivated by greed, and the enemy being supplied by some of our own arms makers. How blind can people be? Are we nothing but puppets to be manipulated by the few? Have we become so beaten down that the people now believe it is futile to fight for equality? I refuse to be a part of such people. I refuse to be a robot.

A beautiful child was running up and down the aisles while his mother was trying to catch him and quiet him down. I caught him up in my arms and started playfully wrestling with him. I assured his mother I wasn't being bothered by him. The child was laughing gleefully. It was the most delicious sound I'd heard in years and years. I looked out the window and saw the fields of grain rushing by, and I pictured myself and the child running with reckless abandon through the fields. Why couldn't life be different? Why couldn't love be the most desired commodity, rather than money and power? The child went back to his mother and soon fell asleep. His mother smiled at me warmly. I wondered at her reaction if she knew I was just released from State Prison. That I was considered incorrigible and extremely antisocial. What a fucked-up world.

The train finally reached Grand Central. I carried the woman's suitcase off the train while she carried the child. Her husband was there waiting and she introduced me as "this wonderful man." The first kind words I heard in God knows how long. They warmed my heart and replaced some of the bitterness. We parted and the magic moment was gone.

89

The full realization of loneliness hit me as I saw the hundreds of people milling about. I had to see my parole officer in the morning and pick up my tickets to California where my parents now lived. I didn't want to live with them but it was the only way they would grant me parole.

I checked into a hotel and lay awake all night wondering what I was going to do. I turned on the TV and watched some show. When it was over, it dawned on me that this was the first whole show I ever saw on TV. Wow, where the fuck have I been, as if I didn't know. I thought of going to California to live with my parents. There wasn't anything I wanted to do, but that was one thing I didn't want to do.

When I saw the parole officer next morning I asked him if I could stay in the city for a few days as I wanted to see my sisters. That wasn't really true, but I needed some excuse. He agreed and said that I was to leave New York within a week. I went to my old neighborhood and the fellows were glad to see me. We went out drinking and some of the guys I had met in prison told me to just be cool and they would cut me into something good. Something was eating at me inside. I was in a very nervous state and I didn't know from what. My body was constantly trembling. It was very strange.

I went up to my sister's and spent the day with her and her husband. It was a very uncomfortable atmosphere. They both left for work the next morning and I had the house to myself. I called up some old girl friends I knew and this one girl agreed to meet me. She was a very pretty girl and though I had tried often to lay her I had never succeeded. I picked her up in a cab and returned to my sister's house. We talked for a bit and then we started kissing. Surprisingly, she allowed me to undress her without any hassle. The first woman I had touched in six years. Wow.

I undressed her slowly, touching each part of her body, and running my hands over her bra and panties. She smelled so good. I sucked her breasts like a starved child, relishing each touch of my tongue on her nipples. I didn't want to leave her breasts but I was anxious to kiss her pubic hairs which were curling out around her panties. I buried my face in her nylon-covered crotch, savoring the female urine taste. Reluctantly I removed her panties and she lay there naked.

I thought of all the fantasies I had in prison of naked women. I licked her whole body, while thinking of all the times I had masturbated in prison fantasizing about her. I licked the crack of her ass, bit her gently on each buttock, and then buried my face between the valley of her buttocks. She was squirming and I was sure no man had made love to her like this. I pushed my tongue deep into her cunt and I wished I had another mouth to lick her breasts at the same time. There was so much I wanted to do but I only had one mouth and two hands. I licked her cunt and she began shaking and jerking. She was moaning wildly now and I felt like a god. My dick was rock hard and I wanted to put it in her, yet I didn't want to quit sucking her pussy.

She was wet as hell now and I buried my nose in the wetness. A real live woman, I thought, not a fantasy. I lay on top of her, aware of every part of our bodies that touched. Her hard nipples pushed against me. I put myself inside her and the warmth of her completely enveloped me. It was like no feeling I had ever experienced before. Suddenly I felt myself come; it seemed as if I was pouring it out. She was moaning wildly, her hips writhing recklessly, and her ankles kicking me in the back. I bent down to suck her breasts and just seconds later I was rock hard again. This time we made love very slowly and I was aware of the explosion building up inside me. I felt it along my entire back and groin. My body began shaking and I came with one big explosion. There couldn't possibly be a better feeling than this in the whole world.

I remained on top of her and licked her face and tasted her spit. I kissed her breasts gently and she caressed my back. We talked quietly and I wished I could remain this peaceful for the rest of my life. She told me no man had ever made love to her as good as I and I felt powerful. Prison hadn't deprived me of that.

She wanted to spend the night with me but I told her I was going out with Al and Mario. She warned me not to, that I might get in trouble. We made love again and as we were getting dressed she said she had a funny feeling something was going to happen to me that night. I laughed it off and promised her I would call in the morning.

As I was putting her in a cab downstairs, again she begged me to be careful. I assured her nothing was going to happen to me, and we could spend the day together tomorrow. She held me tight and gave me a long deep kiss. It was the kind of kiss you might give to someone you don't expect to see for a long time. I felt delighted about her concern for me, though I couldn't understand it. I hadn't the slightest idea of doing anything wrong.

I felt confident of myself as a human being for the first time in years. No one was better than I. They had tried to drum into my head that I was a subhuman, a second-class human, but, shit, I bet not one of those bastards had ever experienced the joy of life and tenderness as I had that day. My body and mind felt completely alive. I was my own man again.

9

I met Al and Mario and we went to a few bars and had some drinks. I thought of my having to leave the city in two days and going to a strange place where I knew nobody. And I would have to put up with my parents' bullshit again. I began experiencing a down feeling. I tuned myself out and listened to Al and Mario telling their war stories; how they got busted and what they got away with, and who got killed and the old neighborhood. I asked Mario if he had a gun, and he told me he kept one in the glove compartment of his car. I remembered how good it was to hold a gun and I decided then to pull one more job. I could use the bread to take to the coast. I had about $200 a friend of mine had given me the night before, along with the plane tickets.

I asked Mario to lend me the gun and also to drive me around until we found an easy score. We drove around until we found an easy score. We drove around we found a quiet dark block with a store still open. It was a clothing store. Mario gave me the gun and I told them to wait down the block, so the car wouldn't get spotted. I walked into the store and I told the old man this was a stickup, and that I didn't want to hurt him. He was a very gentle-speaking man and he said to please take the money and go. I opened the register and took about $20. For some reason I left the rest there. Then I asked him for his wallet saying he had to have more there. He gave me the wallet pleading with me not to take the money in there because he needed it. During all this I had put the gun away.

Suddenly I felt very sorry for him. I thought of him working hard all his life and this was all he had to show for it. A half-ass clothing store. He was even a bigger victim of society than I. And my anger was with society, not a poor slob like him. I gave him back the wallet not taking the money. I told him I was sorry and I hoped I hadn't frightened him too much. He said he wasn't going to call the cops and hoped that I would learn never to do these things again. I left and as I did I heard the wail of distant sirens.

I got in a cab right in front of the place and gave the driver a destination. He was completely unaware of anything happening. About three blocks later I remembered I still had the old man's $20. I stopped the cab, paid the fare and started walking back to the store to return the money. I saw a lot of cops' cars, some driving right by me. I was afraid to turn around and walk back the other way—it might be too suspicious—so I kept walking. For some reason I was sure I could trust the old man not to identify me.

I fingered the .38 in my pocket, feeling the power of it. I told myself I would have no qualms about shooting any cops that stopped me. They were authority and they were brutal bastards. They were my enemy. I felt a strange sense of excitement inside. I wasn't afraid one bit. I hoped that one of the people that fucked me around would try to stop and arrest me. Man! They'd never fuck anyone around again. I saw two men sitting in a car parked at the curb. For a moment I thought of pulling my gun and making them drive me away. But I kept walking figuring I would get lost in the crowd on the next block.

Suddenly I felt a gun shoved in my back and a voice saying, "Put your hands over your head." I hesitated, thinking that I wasn't even going to have a chance to shoot it out. One of them stepped in front of me and I saw this was one of the guys in the car I just passed. With the gun still in my hands I raised my hands over my head. They patted me down searching for a weapon. Neither of the fools saw the gun in my hand. There was nothing nasty about them, they had talked matter of factly, and I couldn't get angry at them. Then I decided to shoot myself. As soon as I reached that decision, one of them spotted the gun and grabbed my arm before I could lower it. They had the gun and everything was over. I felt very disappointed about being wrong regarding the old man. He had called the cops. Shit! what a born loser I was.

They brought me back to the store, and I was surprised when the old man, with a softness in his eyes, said he didn't think I was the person. He said the guy that did it was much taller and much heavier and darker. The cops insisted I was the guy; they even had the gun. But the old man kept shaking his head no. I could swear there were tears in his eyes. They took me to the precinct and there I learned someone else had seen me in the store and called the cops, but they didn't know who the guy was cause he didn't stick around. Despite my predicament I felt greatly relieved that it wasn't the old man. I wasn't wrong about him.

I tried to lie to the cops saying it wasn't me. Why would I stick up such a place when I had $200 and a plane ticket to California? They had taken everything from me during the ride to the station house. They told me what $200? All you had was a plane ticket and about $20. The motherfuckers

95

were going to pocket the rest. I started yelling but they told me to shut up. "You didn't have $200 and if you start lying you did we'll kick your ass." I told them I wasn't going to shut up; one of them stole my money. One of them jumped up and started slapping me. In anger and frustration I swung and punched him right in the face. Immediately, they were all over me kicking and punching me. Soon, I was a bloody mess and hurt all over. They booked and printed me and threw me in a cell.

I felt hopeless and lost. I punched the walls and screamed curses at them. But the cells were situated in such a way that they could barely hear me. What did I do, I asked myself. This is a bad dream. It never happened.

During the ride to court next morning, I heard one cop tell another the old man wasn't going to show up in court. The other cop replied, "No problem. We'll just threaten to arrest him for concealing a crime." Sure enough the old man wasn't in court. For a moment my hopes lifted. Then the cop told the judge he would go get the old man. Soon, the cop comes in with the old man. I could see the look of fear and bewilderment on the old man's face. He looked at me with a feeling of sympathy as if to say, "There's nothing I can do." He was too full of fear of the cops to directly state I wasn't the person, but he did say he couldn't be sure. I knew how bad the old man felt and I felt sorry for him. He was caught up in the system and he was unhappy with himself about it.

I also learned that it wasn't the local cops that first grabbed me. The two that first apprehended me were FBI agents who happened to be in the precinct on an extradition case. When the call came in on the robbery they drove around giving the cops a hand. No wonder they were a bit civil towards me. Even in that my luck was rotten. If it was two of the local cops that grabbed me, they would have done so in a real nasty way, and I'm sure I would have tried to shoot them. My anger and bitterness would have been strong enough to provoke me to do it, not caring whether I lived or not.

So here I was back in jail with a new robbery charge. To make matters worse, the gun they took off me was a policeman's personal gun that had been taken in a burglary months before. They knew I didn't commit the burglary—I was only out of prison five days—but they began pressuring me to find out where I got the gun. I insisted I found it in a garbage pail.

I was taken to the Bronx County Jail, where they hold you while awaiting trial and sentencing. A lot of the guards made cracks and laughed about "that idiot that gets busted for robbery after being out only five days." Each night, in my cell, I wondered where my head was at. Did I have some kind of need for self-punishment? I just about deliberately caused my own arrest. If I didn't feel sorry for the old man, I would have taken his money and split. I could easily have gotten away. In fact I had gotten away. What the fuck was wrong with me? Now here I am, on a new robbery charge, and on top of that I owe four years parole time that I must finish first. God, it will be ten or fifteen years before I ever get free again. Why the fuck did I do this stupid crime? Was it really because I didn't want to go out to my parents? Something has to be wrong with me. And as if the robbery isn't enough to worry about, they're going to hassle me even more because of the "hot gun." They really want to know who ripped off the cop to get the gun. What the hell am I going to do?

I began thinking of playing crazy. If I can get them to think I'm insane, they will have to send me to Matteawan. I can stay there two or three years and come back and get a big break in court. I decided that was the thing to do. I remembered the time before when I tried to hang myself. Yeah, that was it. But how could I do it convincingly with a guy in the cell with me? He would have to call the guard right away, or else it would be obvious I was faking it and he was going along with me. I wondered what I could use to cut my wrist. If I sharpened a piece of metal from my belt buckle that would be good enough. I sharpened it as best as I could. My cell partner was a pretty good guy, so I told him what my plans were and that after I bled pretty much he should start hollering for the guard.

I took the piece of metal and drew it across my wrist. All I got was a slight scratch. I kept hacking away, ripping into the flesh. Several times, it caught on something in my wrist, and I just jerked it, and ripped the flesh. It was coming slowly, and it hurt like hell, but I was determined to do a good job. Better a little pain now than ten or fifteen years in prison. I steadily ripped the flesh open, over and over, and the blood was coming freely now. I took the metal in my left hand and started hacking at my right wrist.

It was beginning to hurt bad now. The blood was all over my left hand and it was hard holding the metal. I wrapped a piece of sheet around the piece of metal, held the corner against my wrist, took a deep breath, and pressing and ripping at the same time laid the skin wide open. The blood was spurting out of both wrists now. I watched the blood and was fascinated with it. I opened and shut my fists for a while to make the blood pump faster. Soon there was plenty of blood over me. My cell partner looked up at me in the bunk and said, "Jesus Christ, you weren't kidding, were you." Then he started hollering for the cop. The cop came down to the cell, saw the blood all over me, and called up the captain.

They took me out of the cell and I kept my head down and refused to say anything. I knew I had to appear as if I was in a deep state of depression. They took me to the hospital where I received over twenty stitches. I had done a pretty good job. The nurses were very nice to me and talked sympathetically too. I felt good about the attention I was receiving.

98

Back at the jail, they stripped me and put me in a cell alone. Next morning, in court, my legal aid lawyer suggested I be sent to Bellevue psycho ward for observation.

Bellevue is a whole story in itself. It is in reality a "Snake Pit." It is made up of a large ward of beds, and a day room. They give you a pair of pajamas to walk around in. There were men there totally insane. Some were walking around talking to themselves, babbling, some were sitting in a catatonic state, and others seemed to have nothing wrong with them. It was far better being there than the county jail. The food was good, you didn't have to lock in in a cell, and there were female nurse's aides. The second day I was there, a doctor called me out and talked to me for about ten minutes. I replied hesitantly, said I didn't care if I lived or died. He said he would talk to me again in a few days. That evening I was told by the guards that I was being discharged and returned to the Bronx County Jail. I couldn't believe it. I hadn't even been there three days. Back at the county jail, I was told if I tried any more stunts I'd get my ass kicked.

A week later I was called to court, and my lawyer told the judge there was no way Bellevue could have any substantial findings on my sanity on the basis of three days. The judge ordered me returned to Bellevue. I didn't talk to anyone. I stayed by myself giving off the impression of depression. In truth this was fairly easy for me, cause I damn sure was depressed. I watched this one guy go into a seizure. They called for the doctor who happened to be a well-built female. She was wearing a short tight skirt, and her breasts were really prominent. She bent and squatted over this guy's face while feeling his pulse. God, if that fool had opened his eyes he could have seen a bird's-eye view of her pussy. Man, she really turned me on. I had heard stories of how she interviewed guys. She would sit with her legs crossed in such a manner it showed her pubic hairs; according to them she

99

didn't wear panties. I watched her as she went around the ward, and she was sure enough a cock teaser. Some psychiatrist.

I had been there a week, still no one had interviewed me. Yet I was being given chloral hydrate, along with everyone else, to sleep at night. I decided I had to do something to draw attention to my "sickness." I waited till the day *she* was on; then I jumped up and started screaming and punching the walls and going into a frenzy (I don't know for sure if this was just an act. I do know I felt like doing it just to get the shit and tension out of me); then I fell to the floor and forced myself to cry. They called for her and she came right over to me and God damn if she didn't squat down asking me what's wrong. I squinted my eyes open and there was her blonde pussy just about a foot from my face. I wanted to crawl in there, but strangely enough not in a sexual way. She was talking very gently and comfortingly to me and I felt like a baby inside. She had me brought to a bed and said I could stay there until I felt better. (Unless a doctor okayed it, we weren't allowed to go by our beds in the daytime.)

The next day she called me out to interview me. Every time she bent over to write something I could see most of her full breasts. Of course she was doing this deliberately. Then she made a big show of crossing her legs and sure enough, I was soon staring at her blonde pussy hairs again. She was looking right at me and knew what I was looking at. She asked me about homosexuality in prison, and whether or not I participated in it. Then she asked me how I felt about being away from females for so much of my life. Her whole interview centered around sex. I responded briefly and reluctantly, as if I was too depressed to talk.

Two or three days later, I was again returned to the county jail. Shit, what the fuck do I have to do to get bugged out. There were guys at Bellevue saner than I that stayed

100

there for months. When I talked to my lawyer about this, he said he had found out the D.A. was convinced I was faking and he wasn't going to let me bug out. Well, I said to myself, we'll see about that.

I had a piece of glass I had picked up and that night I would do a good job. Up on the floor there was this big heavy-set black guy, that claimed he knew karate, and was a professional wrestler. He started fucking with me and told me I better move faster to get on the chow line. I wasn't going to take a chance fighting fairly with him. He had been bullying the tier for some time and my anger towards him had been building up. I waited until he sat down to eat. Even then he sat so solidly in the seat, so I figured I better wait. We had stew that day which I didn't eat. I was too upset. I waited till he was finished and just at the moment he was getting up, halfway out of his chair, I came up behind him and hit him with the hardest right hand I ever threw. I felt a bone crack; I wasn't sure if it was my fist or his jaw. He went down, and all the anger and frustration welled up inside me. I kicked him right in the face, blood spurted from his nose, and still he was trying to get up. I brought my foot back to kick him again and slipped on the stew he had spilled. For a minute I was worried—he damn sure was built like a bull—but as we got up together, all he did was grab me and hold on, screaming for the cops.

They came and broke it up. This was the goon squad that responds to a certain bell that is rung whenever there is trouble. They are all armed with clubs. That punk was crying like a baby when he saw they were going to hit him. They gave him a few slaps and pushed him into his cell. There was one deputy in the group who in recent years has been in trouble because of his brutality towards inmates, and he particularly disliked me. He called me a bunch of names and slapped me right into the circle of the goon squad. I punched the first face I saw and with that the clubs came down all over my head and body. I was beaten to the floor and then dragged into the isolation cell.

My body was really hurting but I felt better inside. I had gotten rid of a lot of feelings inside and the fact that I had fought back reminded me that I was a man no one was going to fuck over. Yet as I lay there wondering what was going to happen to me, the utter hopelessness of my life filled me with desolation. My past was misery and my future was filled with years in prison. I decided no one was ever going to fuck with me again. Death had to be better than this. At least when you are dead you don't feel anything. I just didn't fit into this world. I was tired of being considered and treated like some kind of animal. Not once in my life did someone ever try to find out the real me. At least I cared for people, whereas the people in power didn't give a fuck about anyone. I was through with this life. The more I thought about the idea the more I liked it; it gave me a comfortable feeling. I just knew I wasn't going to be afraid when I cut my wrist, and I was kind of looking forward to watching the blood flow.

I took the piece of glass and very deliberately slashed both wrists several times. Harder and harder till the blood came out thickly and steadily. I lay there calmly and my only thoughts were that I kind of regretted no one was going to give a damn that I was dead. I was laying on a bare spring —they wouldn't give me a mattress—with no shirt, just pants and socks. I was past feeling the springs digging into my back. My hands were on my stomach and I could feel the blood running down my sides. I heard the cop making an unexpected walk around the tier. The flashlight shone in my cell briefly as he walked by, then he doubled back. He called to me and I made believe I was asleep. He aimed the light directly at my body then I heard him running down the gallery. God, I am even a failure at suicide.

102

Soon my door was open and a bunch of guards came in and dragged me out. I heard one say, "Christ, he did a good job this time, the bastard." I felt pretty weak and didn't have the energy to stand, so I just deliberately fell. They wrapped something around my wrists and carried me downstairs to the bullpens, and dumped me on the floor. This one cop— "Blackjack Billy" they called him—told me if he had his way he'd let me bleed to death. I told him "Fuck you" and spit at him. He kicked me in the ribs, but the other guards told him to "Cool it" the ambulance was here. They brought me to the nearest hospital, where I was admitted and given a blood transfusion.

The next day I was returned to the jail. They had told the doctor they were sending me to the psycho ward. Instead I was kept naked in one of the back bullpens for two days. I was filled with pity for myself and what was close to tears the entire time. I had no idea what was going to happen. I didn't want to just stay here like this indefinitely. I started yelling and screaming profanities. Several times they came to the bullpen and told me to shut up. I refused to do so. I wasn't going to be ignored. If I kept screaming they would have to do something. This real rotten captain came to my cell, along with Blackjack Billy, and told me if I screamed again he would "jack" me up. But I couldn't stand feeling nonexistent; I wanted them to know I was alive. I started yelling again.

They came to my cell and handcuffed my arms to the bars overhead. They they wrapped a folded-up blanket around my kidney and rib section, after which they began beating me methodically with blackjacks. Of course, the purpose of the blanket was so the bruises wouldn't be too obvious. I felt as if there were hot pokers inside my kidney area. I began screaming with pain. They stopped, removed the blanket and told me they would be back again if they heard one sound from me.

I was left handcuffed like that all night. I wished I could have willed myself to die. Each time the guard made his rounds I felt a hope that he would uncuff me but he would just walk by. I felt as if I had to piss and I tried to, with no thought that I would be pissing all over my pants, but I couldn't. The burning pain in my kidneys was intense. It was one of the longest nights of my life. I remained like that till about ten in the morning, when this pretty decent Irish captain came by and told one of the guards to uncuff me. I just fell to the floor and lay there curled up from the cold. He threw a blanket in to me and I put it over me. This simple act of kindness made me want to cry.

That evening, when that miserable bastard captain came back on duty he told me he was going to "string" me up again. I told myself anything was better than that and I wasn't going to let him do it. An hour later he came into the bullpen with Blackjack Billy and another guard who carried one of those three-foot-long clubs. They came in matter of factly, not expecting trouble from the way in which I was sitting, with my head down as one in complete despair. As soon as the captain was next to me, I planted my feet and hit him as hard as I could in the general direction of his head. My fist landed right on his cheek. He went down and I jumped up screaming like a maniac. I must have scared the shit out of those two guards, they ran like hell out of the bullpen. I realized I was in a lot of trouble. You just don't hit any guard, much less a captain. I ripped the bandages from my wrists and brutally tore the stitches loose, and blood began pouring out. The guards were coming through the door now, and without thinking I just put my head down and ran it into the steel partition that separated the toilet from the rest of the cell. I felt nothing and when I fell I made believe I was unconscious. One of the guards—I later found out it was

Blackjack Billy—came over and deliberately kicked me in the teeth. I felt my teeth break and I screamed.

The deputy warden in charge of the prison during that shift came by at this moment. I was holding my mouth and blood coming out, my wrists were bloody messes, and I was moaning my head was killing me. I must have looked one hell of a mess. I think I convinced him I had a concussion or something because he told one of the guards to call the hospital and ask for an ambulance. Then he told the civilian male nurse on duty to clean me up. As hurt as I was I almost laughed when they took me to the ambulance outside, because there must have been twenty guards escorting me. I was laid on the stretcher in the ambulance and Blackjack Billy sat next to me. We were followed by a police car, and he kept threatening to throw me out the back door and have them shoot me for attempting to escape.

At the hospital they X-rayed my head although of course I knew there wasn't anything wrong with it. They cleaned up my mouth and my front four teeth were extremely loose; ultimately, I lost them. While the doctor was repairing my wrists, he told the two guards with me that he was arranging for me to be admitted to the psycho ward of a hospital. The cops were telling the doctor he needn't bother, that there was nothing wrong with me, I was just a wise guy. I told the doctor that if he let them take me back to the jail, they would kill me. He started calling all the hospitals to see if they could accept a prisoner on their psycho ward. Of course none could and the doctor was not aware that Bellevue would have to accept me. When the cops finally saw the doctor was not going to allow me to go back to the jail with them, only then did they tell him he could have me admitted to Bellevue psycho ward. After the doctor signed the order, he had to leave the room for a minute. I laughed at Blackjack Billy and called him every name I could think of. I knew he couldn't take a chance hitting me there. In the ambulance he started threatening me, and I spat at him. When he made a move to hit me, the nurse told him he'd better not hit me, or she would make out a full report. When we got to Bellevue, she and the driver got out first. Blackjack Billy was behind me. It was a big step from the ambulance to the ground and rather than step down, I threw myself to the ground, landing on my side, and hollered that he had pushed me. The nurse was furious at him and said she was going to report him. I felt better.

This time I stayed in Bellevue for several weeks. I was thrown out because someone had been tampering with the windows in an attempt to escape and I was suspected. One thing about these nuthouses. If they figure you are trying to escape they ship you right out, on the assumption that you can't be too crazy, if you're trying to get out.

Fortunately, I was not allowed to return to the Bronx County Jail. I had been judged "mentally disturbed" and I could be detained only at Rikers Island Hospital. They had one floor that was the "Mental Observation" floor. I tried to hang myself there, back I went to Bellevue, and after a couple of weeks, back I went to Rikers.

The psychiatrist at Rikers was one of the bravest people I met that worked in a prison. He would not let the officials tell him what to do or how treat his patients. He was 100 percent on my side. I was considered a "hands off case" by the guards. They were told to leave me alone. The doctor was convinced I was insane, and was trying his best to get me sent to Matteawan. I pushed the guards right up to the point that I knew I could get away with. Meanwhile, whenever I went to court, I would carry on like a maniac. My lawyer finally got the court to agree to give me a sanity hearing. Ultimately I changed lawyers, and my case appeared before a new judge,

106

who felt sorry for me and told me if I pleaded guilty he would give me the minimum term. Because I had previous felony convictions I had to receive at least a five-year minimum. He could give me five years to any maximum he chose to impose. I decided to accept the plea of guilty. I was tired from the long hassle and battle, and besides I was sure I could appeal it on the insanity issue.

While waiting for sentencing I was returned to Rikers, and a very tragic event happened there that I shall never forget. This is a realistic picture of just how brutalistic and inhuman the correction department can be. Perhaps in my case they can irrationally excuse themselves for what they did to me on the grounds that I had a long record: I was a criminal, and a wiseguy, an agitator or whatever. But this terrible crime they committed upon a young innocent black boy.

His name, and remember this happened many years ago, and there are hundreds of people whose names I forgot, I can never forget: Ezekiel Patterson, though I nicknamed him Sam Cooke because he sang just like him. He was really one of the most talented people I ever met. Sam had been arrested for fighting with a cop. Sam worked for a meat company and he used to unload meat from the trailers. He was very well built and damn strong. He was a very simple person, extremely honest, open and friendly. He liked people and trusted them immediately. His only living relation was an aunt somewhere.

One night after finishing unloading a truck, he and the fellows drank their usual bottle of wine. Some cops came by and started pushing them around telling them to break it up. One of the cops shoved Sam and he shoved the cop back. Of course they clubbed him and arrested him. He was given ten days on Rikers. I had become very friendly with Sam and liked him a lot. Some of the guys on the tier told Sam he wasn't going to be released but instead, they were going to take him to Bellevue for observation. He really got shook up over this. All he wanted to do was get out, go back to his job unloading meat trucks so he could have some money for Christmas. I told him if they took him to Bellevue he should just play it cool, don't get friendly with anybody and just answer the doctor's questions, and he would get out soon.

The day of his transfer arrived. Unfortunately the cop that brought Sam his personal clothes was a really rotten bastard. Always nasty and threatening. Well, he threw Sam's clothes at him. There was a long rip in the pants and Sam asked if he could sew it up. The cop told Sam to shut up and hurry it up, he didn't have all day. Sam asked once more for time to sew the pants, he really couldn't understand how the cop could refuse him. Sam wasn't aware of the rottenness in some people. The cop got uptight because an inmate dared to answer him back. He pushed Sam saying, "Another word out of you, I'll bust your skull." By the way this officer was also black; you would think he would have some feelings for a young black boy. Sam turned around, and with real innocence, asked the guard why he had to push him. With that the guard shoved him again, this time very hard. Sam pushed back. The guard raised his club, Sam panicked and hit the guard. The guard went flying. Sam was one of the most naturally strong people I've encountered, and unloading those meat trucks certainly made him solid.

The guard ran to the "panic" button and in minutes the floor was filled with guards carrying clubs. The rules strictly forbid the carrying of clubs, but it was a rule completely ignored. They laid into Sam and backed him into a corner. There were so many of the guards they prevented each other from getting in many good shots. Meanwhile, Sam with his fists alone was knocking guards down whenever he connected. Two of them were laid out on the floor and the other

108

guards in their eagerness to get at Sam were actually stepping on the two unconscious guards. For a short while, it was one of the greatest one-man efforts I or anyone else will ever see. Once, when Sam's face was averted to one side, a guard was raising his club to his blind side. I yelled "Look out, Sam" and he instinctively threw a roundhouse right that bounced the guard off the wall and onto the floor. Eventually their numbers overwhelmed him. He went down with them swinging their clubs and daring him to get up. He kept trying to get up, too. But he was hurt too bad. I wished I hadn't been locked in the cell. I damn sure would have joined in and tried to help him, come what may.

They had him laid out on the ground, handcuffed behind his back. The phone rang and suddenly all the guards started running and hiding in the kitchen, some in the female nurses' bathroom. The clubs were hidden in the desk drawer. The elevator door opened and some outside official visitors came onto the floor. All they saw was two guards standing over Sam.

Why the phone rang is this. Whenever official visitors come to the Island, the guard in the ferryboat gate house calls the main office and warns them. The call is then relayed throughout the Island to warn all the guards.

When the visitors asked the guards what happened they said, "Well, this is the Mental Observation" floor and we were transferring this prisoner to Bellevue psycho ward, when suddenly he started attacking us and running into the walls. They may have gotten away with that story; after all, all the visitors saw were two guards. I immediately yelled to the visitors and told them to look in the kitchen and the bathroom. They did, and all the guards came out most sheepishly. The windup was Sam had a fractured skull, two broken hands and some broken ribs. Several guards got into trouble. Tragically, the story doesn't end there. I later learned Sam was sent to a state hospital and while there killed an attendant. Knowing Sam as I did, I know the attendant provoked it. Not a pretty story, is it? No one else may remember Sam, not even those that caused his death, but I shall always remember him.

Since the guards all blamed me for getting the others in trouble, they started making it rough on me. The doctor was doing his best but there was only so much he could do. Finally, one evening, Captain Blood came to my cell. He was really a deputy, but this nickname stuck with him for obvious reasons. He was responsible for severely beating many an inmate and caused the death of several. One of his favorite stunts was to force a man to crawl along a long corridor that lead to the "Bing" (solitary). While the man was crawling, Captain Blood would be beating him with a blackjack in each hand. He was feared and hated by every inmate. One story is that someone had turned his daughter into a junkie, and that's why he was such a maniac. That story was never proven.

This evening he came to my cell with some other guards. The cell door opened and he told me to come out. I knew something terrible was up. There's no reason for them to open a cell at night unless there's going to be trouble. I refused to come out. He warned me if I didn't come out they would use tear gas. "Fuck it," I said, "I've been gassed before." They sprayed the gas in and came in with gas masks on. I was tightly handcuffed and brought to another building where the punishment cells are. Captain Blood had had holes drilled through the sides of the metal bunk so he could handcuff unruly prisoners. I was stripped and cuffed to the bunk. This was retaliation for ratting on the guards that day.

He came into the cell, along with the captain from the Bronx County Jail that I had knocked out (he had been transferred to Rikers), looked down at me, and very coldly and deliberately said I was not going to leave this Island alive. I could forget about the doctor helping me now. Then they left. I wasn't too worried, just angry. I knew the doctor would have me released when he came on in the morning. Early the next morning, Dep. Hawk-nose came into the cell. He stood alongside the bunk, looked down at me and said soon I would get what was coming to me. I had been having to piss for hours and was holding it in. While he was running his threats to me, I turned just slightly and let go. Before he realized what was happening and jumped back, I had gotten some pretty solid streams all over his pants. He cracked me in the face with the sides of his hands. Repeating his threats, he left.

I started getting a little scared. Something was wrong. Something was very strange. I wondered why the doctor hadn't been over to find out what happened. A short time later, Mr. Russell, the guard that worked in the receiving area, came to my cell. Without a doubt he was the most humane guard on the Island. He always had a special liking for me. He explained to me what had happened. Captain Blood had left on the doctor's desk a transfer paper stating that I had been sentenced and transferred to Sing Sing. My name was off the count in the hospital. Of course the doctor believed it; there was no reason he shouldn't, and it would never dawn on him that the Dep. would do what he was doing. Russell told me that in effect I had been kidnapped from the hospital part of the Island. There was no way the doctor could know I was in this part. Oh God. Now I could understand why they felt so sure of themselves. Of course, they could do anything they wanted to with me.

Russell told me he was sending word to the doctor where I was, but I better never say to anyone what he was doing for me. If the Deps ever found out, it would be all over for him. He would get every shit detail on the Island. I assured him no one would know. An hour later, the doctor came to my cell, ordered the cuffs removed and brought me back to the hospital building. There was little he could do to the Dep. and I guess he knew it was futile to even try. I do know I wasn't bothered again while I remained on the Island.

I was sentenced to five to seven years in state prison. The parole department would make me do two years of my violation first, and then I started the five-to-seven-year term. I won my appeal on the grounds that I had requested and was granted a sanity hearing, but never received one. There was obviously a great deal of question on my sanity during the proceedings that led up to my pleading guilty. Seven more long years were taken from my life, and once more I was returning to the streets a bitter angry man.

10

A thousand books could be written on the inhuman atrocities committed in prison, all in the name of society's correctional methods. After reading these books feelings would differ. Some readers would disbelieve such things could happen in our great society. Some readers would sympathize and say "What a shame," "Something should be done." Some would say, "It can't be as bad as all that, the writer must be exaggerating," and still others would say, "They deserve even worse."

But no one, unless he has been in prison, no matter how detailed the books may be, will be able to "feel" these atrocities. They'll never know what it is like to have to live with such incidents seared into the mind. Perhaps it's best that way. Otherwise millions more people would be harboring a hate and distrust in humanity. Millions more people would be disillusioned in a society that lives by double standards.

I am going to write of a few—just a few—such senseless atrocities. I shall do no exaggerating. There is no need to do so. The truth is more brutal than I could have dreamed up.

113

There was a young fellow I knew named Tommy. He was serving a 25-year term for robbery. He had committed no violent crime ever. Well, one day Tommy passed out in the yard. He was brought up to the hospital. A male nurse, O'Keefe, as rotten and sadistic a person as possible, had him placed in the "Bug Cell" (a psychiatric observation cell) completely stripped. O'Keefe justified doing this on the pretext that Tommy had faked fainting. Tommy was released several days later from the cell, thoroughly frightened. He knew how easy it was for these people to ship you to the Bughouse.

A week later Tommy passed out again. There were three of us present and we decided we better not take him to the hospital right away. We would wait and see if he woke up shortly. We laid him on a bench and after a bit he came to. We knew something was terribly wrong with him, so we spoke to one of our friends that worked up in the hospital. We told him we wanted Tommy's temperature taken without O'Keefe knowing. If his temp was normal O'Keefe wouldn't know anything about his being up there. If he had a temperature then O'Keefe would have to make out a report and do something. Of course, we were aware that just because a temperature was normal that did not mean nothing was wrong with Tommy. Well, anyway Tommy had a very high temperature. O'Keefe couldn't just dismiss it because the inmate that took the temp also gave a copy of it to the inmate secretary of the doctor.

Tommy was admitted to the hospital. For two months they could not find out what Tommy was suffering from. It became obvious Tommy was real sick. They gave him all kinds of medicine, but nothing happened. Tommy began waking up in the morning with blood all over his teeth gums and lips. Finally, they decided to take some further tests. Tommy had leukemia and died shortly after.

His family had made an appeal to the authorities to allow

114

Tommy to die at home, free from stone walls and prison guards, where his remaining days could be spent in loving care. The authorities refused. And O'Keefe still wasn't through. The morning Tommy died, his family was there. Tommy was having difficulty breathing. The doctor ordered an oxygen tank hooked up. O'Keefe brought one into the room and hooked it up. An hour or two later it was found to have been an empty one. I was there in the hospital with Tommy, one of the most gentle, giving people I'll ever know.

It's interesting to know how I got admitted to the hospital at that time. I was scheduled to be discharged from the prison soon but I had bone chips on my elbow that were giving me hell. The doctor had ordered some kind of treatment designed to melt them. O'Keefe was in charge of this machine. When he saw the chips, he said the machine wouldn't help, and it would be an easy thing to just cut them out. He said he could do it in just a few minutes, it was that simple. I could feel they were right under the skin, so I figured it had to be a minor cut. What I didn't know was that he was not authorized to do it. Anyway he cut my elbow open, and cut out some of the bone chips. I returned to my cell. About a week later the incision opened up and a bad infection had started. As I said I was going home soon, and they don't want anyone to go home with a medical problem. They admitted me to the hospital.

During this same period in the hospital there was a black guy named Turk who had broken his leg. They had put it in traction and he had a cast on the ankle. I used to stop in his room and rap with him. He told me his ankle was killing him. When he complained to O'Keefe all he got was a shitty grin. "O'Keefe's trademark." He told O'Keefe something was wrong with the traction, because the pain was terrible. O'Keefe laughed at him and said all he was doing was trying to get extra pain medication.

115

Finally the one decent doctor of the three came on rounds. Turk convinced him something wasn't right. The doctor got cast cutters and cut a piece of the cast away. God, the stench was nauseating; the flesh had rotted from lack of blood circulation. After they cut all the cast away the sight was sickening. Almost all the flesh on his foot from his toes to his ankle had rotted away; each of the bones were clearly visible. Christ, I'll never forget that. A few days later I was released from prison, so I never found out if his foot had to be amputated.

Can your stomach stand another? This also involves O'Keefe. In fact it is a case of homicide. There was a fellow Charlie that had an operation. Afterward someone had to sit by his bed ready to operate the suction machine so Charlie didn't suffocate choking on the fluids in his lungs. Things were going well until O'Keefe came on duty. He didn't dig sitting by an inmate's bed for eight hours, when he could be up front in the office fucking around. So he spent most of the time up front rapping. When the 12 o'clock shift came on, Charlie was dead!

In a lighter vein, I'll explain what happens at sick call in the morning. There is this one doctor, a refugee who speaks broken English. You go up to him and say you have a pain in your chest. He tells you to quit smoking. You reply you don't smoke. He tells you the pain is from tension, and you should smoke to relax! I swear it is the truth. You complain of a pain in your back. He tells you to quit lifting weights. You tell him you don't lift weights. He then tells you to start lifting. "It's good for you." I could go on and on.

11

The train arrived at Grand Central and as I got off, I quickly noticed nothing had changed. The people were still the same, rushing around, as rude as ever, banging into you without a backward glance, the same cold looks on their faces. I walked around the streets for a while experiencing my freedom. There was no particular place for me to go. I certainly wasn't going up to my sister's in the Bronx. I walked up Lexington Avenue and it seemed every ten steps there was a prostitute. I was damn sure horny, but I had never dug having to pay a girl for sex.

I kept walking and I began feeling very lonely. There was no one in the whole city that even cared if I got hit by a car, much less that I just got out of prison. Everyone seemed to have a place to go. I came upon a very old woman sitting on the steps of a now closed store. She was flanked by two shopping bags. Her clothes were old and raggy. She too obviously had no place to go. I felt for her. What a tragic thing to be old and alone and no home. I wanted to say something to her. I wanted to let her know someone knew a little of how she felt. More important I wanted to let her know I wasn't part of the cold rat race that exiled her to this doorstep. I walked over and asked how she felt. They just didn't seem the right words but what else could I say. She looked up at me with a glare and said, "Leave me alone, go away. What do you care how I feel," and she clutched her shopping bags closer to her side, as if I might steal them.

I walked away from her, my feelings of sympathy turning to disgust and hate at a society that reduced people to this. Not trusting anyone, not even a stranger with a kind word. To her no one cared, and there had to be something suspicious if someone tried to be nice to her. "What a rotten fucking world," I thought to myself. "God, I don't want to end up like that. I'd rather get killed taking my chances stealing a lot of money."

I walked towards a hotel glittering a few blocks ahead. I was filled with anger and confusion. I felt so completely alien toward all these other people walking along the streets. A pretty young girl approached me and asked if I wanted a good time. She looked about seventeen. She spoke quietly and I felt akin to her, so I agreed. But she would have to come with me to the hotel I was checking into. "Okay with me," she replied. I began getting sexually aroused, and feeling good. At least I wasn't alone. I would have love even if it was paid for.

Up in the room she undressed and I insisted she had to take a shower with me. I began asking her the usual questions, How long she was hustling and what got her into it. I got the usual put-off answers. In bed I began kissing her breasts and moving my hands over her lush body. Nothing was happening. I couldn't get a hard on. She turned around in the bed and began sucking my prick. Nothing! Absolutely nothing! I tried concentrating on women that had aroused

118

me in the past. It didn't work. After a while she turned and asked me what was wrong.

Rather than hurt her feelings which I may have if I explained about her being a prostitute, I told her I just got out of prison and I guess it would take a while getting readjusted. She asked me about prison, how long I was in for, and why I went, and I could sense at that moment she felt for me. She was far from the cold hard prostitutes. We talked for a while and I felt very warm and friendly toward her. She began fondling me in an effort to get me aroused but still no success. She stayed with me for about an hour and a half. I told her I would come down this way again and look for her and perhaps take her out to dinner. And that if she ever needed help I would be glad to help her. I didn't feel alone again. I realized there were lots of people with unfortunate lives. I wasn't the only one. In fact, I was better off than most, because I could handle the hurt better than they. I was more callous and tougher inside than they.

I went up to see my parole officer in the morning. He dictated the rules to me in a cold unfriendly way. He assured me he was going to keep a close eye on me and the first time I fucked up that would be it. I had to report every week and tell him where I was working. I quickly found out he had a bad reputation. He would violate someone every week. He wasn't the type you could talk to. In fact I had to lie to him the very first day. When he asked me to account for the money I left the prison with the day before, I had to tell him I gave a cab driver a $20 bill by mistake. I had spent $60 for the room and dinner and the girl. He would have hassled me about spending the night in a hotel and he could have violated me if I admitted having a girl up in the room. While on parole one wasn't allowed to sex with anyone but his wife. He called me a damn fool about giving the cabby $20 by mistake and I better grow up fast. I was sure glad to get out of that office.

I went to see my sister and her kids. I dug the kids but I was never close to my sister, so after telling her and the kids if the parole officer ever calls just tell him I'm either working or went to a movie, I checked in a cheaper hotel with the last few dollars I had. I looked up some old friends and asked if they could get me a job. They said they would look around. Meantime I started work in a factory. It was a real dull draggy job.

I moved in with a friend of mine in a garden apartment. We had a ball. I guess it was one of the nicest times of my life. Free, unhassled, and peace of mind. We didn't worry about money. In fact he collected unemployment and would be broke the day after. Likewise with my paycheck. We had lots of girls staying over. We'd drink, smoke grass, eat Chicken Delight, and fuck. The neighbors soon called our apartment "Peyton Place." We had lawn parties and we would all be half undressed. I began staying away from work more and more, till finally I just quit. Of course I didn't tell the parole officer.

There was a beautiful girl living next to us and we were all good friends. I began really digging her, but she had lots of boy friends and liked to go out. I took her to the local bar a few times and told her I really dug her and she better forget about anyone but me. She laughed. One night one of her boy friends was staying over. I decided I'd make it a bit difficult for them. I knocked on her door and asked for some sugar. About an hour later I knocked and asked for some coffee. She was getting a bit angry by now. I climbed the tree opposite our apartment to get her a bouquet of flowers that bloom on the tree. When I got up the tree I realized the flowers curl up at night into shells. Fuck it, I'll give them to her anyway. So I knocked on the door and hollered I had to see her. When she opened the door I handed them to her. She took them and hit me in the head with them. I'll tell you, they hurt too.

After that I started sitting on her stoop and when one of her dates called for her I'd say she was out. He'd seem a bit surprised but what else could he do. It wasn't too long before most of them began thinking we were making it together. Two or three others I had to downright threaten and tell them I better not see them around any more. I told her they couldn't be worth a shit if they didn't stand up to me. They must not have thought her important enough. By now she was taking it in good spirits. We were together most every night.

Meantime, a friend of mine got me a job bridge painting. The pay was great and I enjoyed the danger of going up high. I was really killing myself though. I'd drink and get high and fuck every night till 3 or 4 in the morning. Then the guy driving me to the job would call for me at 6. I certainly was in poor shape to do high work. One morning I didn't wake up until about 10 or 11. And where was I? Atop a 60-foot-high pipe. I had ridden to the job and got up the pipe to paint in an unconscious state.

There was a whole gang of us on the job and we all got paid in cash. I noticed the payroll would be delivered with two guys in a car. I started thinking how easy it would be to take them off. I found out the office from where they brought the money. Then I quit the job. I bought a gun and told my friend about the easy touch and asked if he wanted in on it. Of course he agreed.

The next Friday we watched them come out of the office with the box full of pay envelopes. We followed them out to the job. There didn't seem to be any good place for the stickup. I knew the driver had a gun, but they were very loose and unsuspicious. I decided the only fairly decent place to do it was right outside the office. We wouldn't be able to go to our car because that would leave them yelling and screaming for the cops. We'd hit them just when they were getting into their own car, and we would drive off in their car. My friend was leery, but I told him not to worry, I'd handle it.

The next Friday I was ready. I felt good inside. The excitement building up. I felt alive! I fondled the gun and felt the power it gave. I stuck it in my belt and it felt as if it was made to be there. I stationed myself at a place where when they came out the door to the car at a casual pace I would meet them, just at their car. I told my friend to stay put until I had them getting into the car. Then he was to come over to drive the car away. I had to be sure to catch the driver with the keys in his hand. I didn't want to chance having to depend on him getting them out of his pocket.

They came down the steps and I started walking. The driver first opened the door on the passenger side to let the guy with the money box in the car. Then he strolled around to the driver's side. Meantime the guy in the car reached over and opened the door for the driver. Just as the driver was pulling open the door I was two steps away.

I called very matter of factly, "Hey Mister, can you tell me . . ." He turned unsuspectingly to hear my question. I showed him the gun and said very quietly, "Don't do anything stupid. It's not your money." To convince him I made a show of cocking the gun. I told him to get into the back seat with his hands in sight at all times. I got in behind him and by now my friend was ready to get in the driver's seat. Everything worked perfect. What luck! No one had noticed a thing. I knew I had taken a hell of a chance, but it paid off.

I took the driver's gun and we drove to a section of the city we had already picked out where they would be unable to call for help. We dropped them out of the car and drove to our own car. Home free with a little more than 10 grand. Wowee! It was about time for me to live it up. The money went fast. I bought a secondhand car and lots of expensive clothes, along with a watch and ring.

Things were going nice for me. I was frequenting nice bars where the girls began knowing me. I had worked out a deal with my so-called "conscientious" parole officer. I would give him $20 a week and he wouldn't hassle me. I hated giving that bastard the money but I had no choice.

I met this guy named Pete through some good people. He needed someone to take off this junkyard where it would be an easy 5 grand. I agreed to go with him. We parked the car around the corner, went in and stuck the place up. We locked the owners in the office and left, not thinking much about the black guys that worked there. As we ran to the car they started hollering. It was my car we were using and I worried about them getting the plates. We got about a block from the house we were heading for, when the driver goes through a stop sign accidentally. Sure enough, just as we pull up to the house the cops pull up alongside us. He shows them his license and I have to explain the car is registered in my girl's name and they can call if they doubt it.

At this moment the call comes through on their radio. Three guys, white, driving a green Thunderbird robbed a junkyard. My car was blue but with the dust all over it, it could be mistaken for green unless you were up close to it. The cops know something is up. Pete tells the cops, "Listen, you both know Billy. He'll tell you we are okay. He is inside now."

Meantime, I am scared to death. I got a loaded .38 on me and the stolen money. I am debating just when I should pull out my gun and make a break for it. These guys ain't got no record, they don't know what jail is like and if I get caught it's all over for me. Pete catches my eye, and his expression tells me, "Don't worry." Fat chance. I'm not going to just let them get me this easy.

One of the cops follows Pete into the house, so I follow behind him. I am in a better position now than just standing in the street with the other cop. When we go into the house Pete brings the cop into the room where Billy is. I headed for the kitchen and out the window. I went through the back yards and on up the avenue. A half hour later I call Billy not knowing what to expect. He tells me I almost fucked things up by splitting with the dough, but he finally made the cop agree to getting his cut later. I knew Billy ran numbers for some big people, and only later did I find out just how many cops from that one precinct were taking payoffs.

At any rate, I swore then, I was going to stick to my old promise of not sticking up any more legitimate people. I couldn't hassle the chance of getting caught and going through the courts. I knew my next sentence would be a big one, and I was all too aware I wouldn't get no kind of fair trial. If the cops and D.A. don't have you right, they get the witnesses to lie, and I couldn't deal with that shit any more. I'd wait for a good crap game to take off. I'd much rather risk getting killed than going back to prison. And with a little caution, no one would know who took off the game or where to find them. Plus, since I would be doing such risky stuff I'd be ever alert and make it pretty hard for anyone trying to get me.

So I just played it cool, hung around, shot pool at the bar, and fucked every girl I could. It was a pretty easy life. By now I was living with Marian, the girl from next door. We had a rather expensive apartment in a good neighborhood. She was still working every day. I really dug her, yet I would be out just about every night. She knew I was doing something wrong, and she even told me she would be willing to support me if I would stop fucking around.

I cared very much for her, and I knew she loved me. I hated hurting her, yet I just had to go out at night. Life was too dull unless I was living a fast life. This has always plagued me. Nor was I able to deal with a close meaningful relationship. After being in prison so many years, never revealing much of yourself, it becomes your nature to keep your feelings stuffed. I would have killed for her, and yet I wouldn't stay home at nights with her.

Usually I would sleep most of the day and still be home when she got in from work. Then when she saw me getting dressed to go out she would go in the bedroom and start crying. I couldn't deal with it. We never fought, although she had one hell of a temper. She would just cry, and I would feel like a real bastard. But still I would promise her after this deal went off we would go away somewhere and I wouldn't fuck around any more. Many times if I got home at four or five in the morning, I'd find her sitting up in the bed sleeping with the TV on. She had been waiting for me.

Despite my always running out, I'm sure she knew I really did care for her, and that I was driven by a compulsion. I feel now the only crime I committed in my life was what I did to her. Can a man be so driven that he doesn't do the things he really wants most? I certainly wanted her love more than anything. Looking back at my relationship with her and some other girls, I think I doubted their love, and I would keep putting them through a test waiting till they got fed up and left. Then I could say, "I knew it; she never really loved me." Since I couldn't deal with it, I would drive it away.

To avoid seeing her cry when I left each night, I started leaving before she came home. And that became the pattern.

We would have Saturday and Sunday afternoons together. Generally we spent them in bed making love. Our lovemaking was terrific. I have always been a fantastic lover, giving more concern about pleasing my partner than to myself. I guess because I was deprived of women for so long I appreciate their bodies more than other men. Reaching a climax is not the biggest thrill for me. Bringing the woman to a climax is far more important because I know I will have one. I guess this attitude has helped me immensely in always having lots of women.

Just about this time I came close to getting my ass in big trouble. I had been playing poker at this club. On nights when three tables were in use, perhaps there was maybe 10–15 grand in the place. It was on the street level in an old storefront. It seemed like a real easy score. Of course, I wouldn't be able to go in myself.

I really disliked trusting someone else to do the actual sticking up. I knew I was able to judge the situation better than others. I knew when to talk calmly, and when to threaten. Most times if you talk calmly the victims will comply, but if you use force or scare them too much they panic and are liable to do something crazy which causes the whole thing to blow up. I figured this game would be a simple job and I would drive the getaway car. That way I'd still be on top of things.

I set the game up with two friends of mine. They would wear stockings over their heads to make identification difficult. I told them to strip everybody and take the jewelry too. They had plenty of time. No one would come in by surprise. The door had to be opened and while one guy held the shotgun on the players the other could very easily open the door and let anyone in.

I waited in the car, a little apprehensively. There was a chance someone passing in the street would recognize me, so I had my face kind of buried. There were no sounds coming from the place so I knew things were going smoothly. Soon they came out and got in the car. I pulled away and turned the first corner and drove moderately. They told me there were only about ten guys in the place and only one table was in use. Shit, what rotten luck. Every other Wednesday there were generally twenty to thirty cats in the place. We split the bread up and it came to about two grand apiece. Hardly worth the effort.

I should have gone right back to the game the next day. This would have allayed any suspicions. About two weeks later word came to me that the guys down at the game wanted to see me. I figured I better show and bluff it out. Along with my pistol, I put a hand grenade in my coat pocket. I pulled up in front of the place and no sooner was I out of the car, I was surrounded by some very angry people. "You son of a bitch, you took off the game," Tony yelled. "We know it was you. That's why you haven't been around. Don't worry, you're going to be taken care of." And as he was saying this he raised his hand to slap me. I couldn't afford to be meek and defensive. I couldn't act as if I was scared. I was going to bluff this out right down the line.

I stepped back, and screamed back at them. "Listen you bastards, why would I take off the game? It wouldn't be worth it to me, I generally carry more money than all of you have in the game." They couldn't know the truth to this last remark. All they knew was that I usually carried a roll of bills. "Would I be stupid enough to go in there where you all know me?" "We know you didn't come in yourself, but you set it up. And you're gonna get it."

I could sense though, that now there was a little doubt in their minds. I had to push my point now to let them know if they started any shit there was going to be a lot of trouble over something they weren't too sure of. I told them very

127

firmly I was no patsy, and if I heard there was a contract out for me, which I would because I knew a lot of people, I was coming down there and blow the whole fucking place up. For emphasis, I pulled the hand grenade out of my pocket and flipped it up in the air and caught it. I told them they didn't know where I lived, I could come from behind parked cars, out of the sewers, they would never know where I was coming from. But I would always know where to find them. They had to be here every day. This is where they took care of their business and it would be so easy for me to come by some Saturday or Sunday when all their kids and wives would be around, and just throw a few grenades.

Their reaction to this almost started a war right there. But I had my hand on my gun, and told them a bit more nicely that I didn't take the game off, and I wasn't going to stand here denying it all night, and they could believe what they want. With that I got in my car and drove away. I later found out that they believed maybe I didn't take the game off, but I better stay out of their neighborhood and if I started any shit, they'd get me. Two days later, I moved to another apartment, just in case. It was essential no one knew where I lived in this business.

12

I awoke from one of the best sleeps I ever had. The sun was shining brightly and a warm breeze from the ocean came in through my open windows. I could see the Throgs Neck Bridge, even from my bed. I stretched luxuriously, feeling rich and complacent, and a deep thrill of anticipation filled my head. I reached over and picked up my gun, enjoying the feel of it. I laid it on my stomach, reveling in the power it seemed to give. Tonight was finally going to be payoff night. Long weeks of hassling, hustling, aggravation, and frustration were finally culminating. Tonight was going to be the night.

The excitement filled me with a warm, deep-centered sexual feeling. For a moment I wished my woman hadn't gone to work this morning. I lay there, not in any rush; I had a few hours to get ready. It was now only four in the afternoon. On impulse, I picked up the phone and called Mary. Her husband was at work, and I knew she would be just laying around the house. I hadn't seen her since I moved from her block, but it was obvious she really dug me. The few nights we were together, she threw herself into me. Hi Mary, surprised to hear from me? Listen, I'll call a cab for you, and why don't you come on over. You haven't seen my new place. No, don't worry, Marian won't be home till late tonight. She is going to a company party. Okay, great, I'll expect you in a half hour.

I got up and took a shower, smoked some grass, and lay back. I allowed myself to think back how this whole score started. A little more than two months ago. Up until then, I had been ripping off a few bookies, never getting more than a few thousand, and most times a lot less. Life was good since I got out of jail. Sleeping all day, nightclubbing, and gambling in the after-hours joints. But still I felt I was missing out on something. There were few thrills in what I was doing. The excitement wasn't as good any more.

Then one evening, I started rapping with Richie, one of the fellows that hung out in Tony's, a cool hangout for various groups into many different hustles. It was a safe place—the local precinct was on the take. I myself was paying off four or five cops, and I knew other groups were paying off also. It was a nice quiet place, where each respected the other's privacy. When a group was rapping at one of the tables, they knew no one would come over and cut in. It was a very impressive place also, clean, good Italian food, and a congenial atmosphere. I was well known by all, but none really knew what I was doing. They knew I was a stickup man, or rather they surmised it, because of my reputation from the past. But for sure, they certainly didn't know I was ripping off bookies or crap games. I wouldn't have lived too long if they had known that, since they were all connected in some way with the mob.

Me and Richie had rapped a few times in the past each trying to feel the other out, so to speak. He always kidded me

130

about all the girls I brought in there. Well, this night, after about an hour of rapping, he asked me point out, how'd I like to make about a hundred thousand dollar score. Of course I said sure, even though mentally I was saying to myself, another exaggerated deal. Every time I was supposedly cut into a big score, it never turned out anywhere near it was supposed to be. But that was one of the things a stickup man lived with and expected.

Richie said he knew I was a crazy bastard with too much heart, but him and his friends had been thinking about cutting me in for some time now. I knew his friends, but I never knew what their gig was. They always seemed to have money and were driving big cars. They weren't into junk, I felt, because although they rapped with the junk crowd that hung out in Tony's they weren't part of them. The same went with the gambling crowd.

Richie started out by telling me he had heard I was suspected of taking off the game down at the Club. He knew that it was straightened out, but between us, he felt sure I did it. But he most dug the strong way I came on, when I was confronted with the fact. So he felt he knew that I didn't have any qualms or fears about taking members of the mob off. Naturally, I wouldn't admit anything to him, not that I had any reason not to trust him, but at the same time, I learned never to trust anyone. So I let him do the talking. They knew a guy they could take off for a hundred thousand, and they needed a guy like me to help them, cause they were too well known to the guy, and couldn't get near him with a gun, plus they didn't want to get identified by the cat.

Immediately, I knew it was a mob figure they were after. To me it didn't matter. In fact it was the ideal thing to me. I had long ago decided not to ever rob a legitimate man again. I couldn't hassle with the courts with my record, and

I preferred death to further imprisonment. Taking off racket guys, at least I wouldn't be turned in to the cops. If I got caught, I'd be killed.

Richie didn't give me the whole setup then. I guess he had a natural hesitancy to trust me also. I learned the whole thing as I got involved into it. Richie and I agreed to meet later with his two partners, Veto and Louie. But not in this place. They never discussed their deals even amongst themselves in this place. If the slightest word was heard, they would be uptight, since everyone else in the place was connected in some way.

After meeting with Veto and Louie, we split up in two cars and went to Connecticut, and looked over the house where Carmine lived. It was a sumptuous place, at least in the hundred-thousand-dollar bracket, with lots of trees and bushes and a long driveway. A very quiet street and it wouldn't pay to loiter at all around there. The cops patrolled the streets frequently. The plan was to follow him constantly and pick the best place to kidnap him. As yet we had no idea just where that place would be.

Our tipster was one of the mob himself. In fact a very well-respected person, who was well known to Carmine. The tipster's name was T. I didn't dwell on why he was setting up these people, other than the fact he probably needed bread, plus he was a cousin to Richie. Contrary to what most people believe, even those connected don't always have bread. The big guys, sure have loads of it, but there are many that have to get into a hustle themselves. Obviously whatever T was into, it wasn't enough for him. Then too, as I later learned, he was really loyal to another family, whose idea was to create fear and distrust amongst Carmine's family.

Each night T would have a number where one of us could be reached, and he would call and tell us where Carmine was and any plans he had, if any. Generally, Carmine, like all the other bosses, was a night person. They would meet at a club in the evening, sit around and talk, go to a spot for a drink, get the reports on the day's activities, and often wind up the night at a private gambling spot mostly for friendly gambling. He would head home somewhere about two or three in the morning. Overall, this was his routine, interspersed with a night out on the town with some glamor girl and some friends. He would move around a lot, though, in the neighborhood.

Our problem was to decide where would be the best place to take him, with the least chance of creating a disturbance. It was further complicated by the fact that many nights, rather than going home, he would go to his girl friend's house, which was also in Connecticut. On top of that, many nights he would be accompanied by a friend, besides his bodyguard-chauffeur. We hoped to catch him on a night when he would be driving the car himself. Some of these bodyguards might do something foolish, and fuck everything up for us. If we made an attempt and blew, we wouldn't be able to try again, for he would be on the alert.

So practically every night we had to take turns following him, in two and sometimes three different cars. Each of these cars had to be rented cars, and we would change them continuously. If we used our own cars and we were spotted, it wouldn't be difficult for them to check the registration from our plates. We had a Central Police number we could call, and a cop that was on the take would give us the name and address of the owner of any license plates we phoned in. Naturally we knew the mob had this number also, or a connection of their own. Nor could we risk having our faces spotted, especially Richie and Veto, for they were well known to most of the racket guys, being somewhat in it themselves.

Our nights usually consisted of getting a call from T,

which in some cases took hours; then we would go to the place where Carmine was and park a few blocks from the joint. Normally we would spot his car, but again sometimes he would be using someone else's. We would have to watch close for him to come out, and see which car he got into. Some nights he wouldn't travel out of the neighborhood; other nights, we had to follow him all over the city, and sometimes Jersey. It wasn't easy. Many times, we lost him, because we had to be sure not to get too close. Generally one of our cars would try to get in front of him and one behind. Many times we had three cars, and the two behind would play leapfrog with each other, to insure not getting spotted. These racket guys were very cagey, being aware of the chances of getting taken off, or of being followed by the agents, or even getting killed by another family.

We had to do this just about every night, so that eliminated most of our chances of a social night out. If we lost him early enough and couldn't pick him up again, generally I had a few girls' numbers I could call for a late evening date. But this was costing money between renting all these cars, and the motel room we had to keep paying for in the event we kidnapped him on any given night. I was in to a shylock for a bit now, and was anxious to get this over with. It was getting to be real hard work. Each night we thought this would be the night, only to be confronted with some new obstacle.

I was getting irritable and kind of disgusted with the others. It seemed to me they were being too careful. And they were afraid. I began to see why they needed me. In a way they were using me, but I didn't particularly mind. Just as long as it led to some big dough. If I could have set something like this up myself, I would have done it, but too many connections were needed. Plus you just couldn't find guys that were willing to take the risk doing things like this. Those same dopes would think nothing of sticking up some legit guy and risk having a thousand police after them, and a long jail term. Yet they were afraid to risk death. Long ago I realized I had a far better chance hassling with the mob than with the police. And if a contract went out on me, I had as much chance of getting them as they had me. This is how I felt, and believed.

One night, T called us and said we should be able to do for sure this night. Carmine was going out to Jersey, to see someone in a few minutes. He was going out there alone. We could get to the place about the same time as him, since he was going through the Lincoln Tunnel and we could take the Washington Bridge. We left hurriedly, but couldn't take the risk of speeding on the turnpike, lest we be stopped. Each of us had a gun along, plus rope and tape. We were anxious and felt this was it. We figured to get him as he came out of the house where he was visiting. We were familiar with the neighborhood as we had been out there several times. It was dark enough out and the section was fairly well deserted. Louie and I would get him from behind, put a pair of taped-up sunglasses on him (the wraparound kind), throw him into the car and then tie him up. We knew he probably wouldn't make a sound, because these people would rather pay the money than take any chance of getting hurt or killed.

We had to do all this without him seeing our faces. If he spotted us, we had to kill him. There was no other way. The main reason we didn't want to kill him was that then anyone we took after that would realize they were going to get killed and therefore wouldn't cooperate with us. Plus his partner would figure, why come up with the ransom, since they'll kill him anyway. We checked everything out and made arrangements how to go about getting him back to New York, through the tollbooths and all. We would take him to the motel while Richie would make the phone call to his partner, and make arrangements about the payoff.

135

I wanted to have full knowledge about the payoff part, because I still didn't fully trust anyone. I even anticipated killing the other three and keeping the whole hundred thousand myself. That way I would have enough bread to retire on, and I would never have to worry about anyone ever opening up. I let the thought stay in my head, and figured I would make the positive decision if and when the opportunity of getting them all together presented itself. I had no qualms about it for several reasons. Each of them had already been in on a few murders, plus if they had reason, they wouldn't hesitate to kill me. More important I strongly felt you live by the sword and expect to die by the sword.

When we reached the house, we saw he was there already. The car T told us he was driving was in the driveway. Me and Louie snuck up to the house and laid in the bushes, gun in hand. It was pretty dark, so chances of getting spotted were very unlikely. And we waited, and we waited, for two hours, three hours, going on four hours. The fellows in the car occasionally passed by to see if everything was okay.

Laying in the bushes waiting for what seems an interminable period of time, with the ground getting colder and colder, we didn't dare make a sound, knowing that any given moment, any number of things can happen. Maybe we have been spotted by those in the house, and they have called for some goons to come get us. This causes you to be very anxious and alert about not just the house or the road, but also every area around you; the slightest noise bears investigation. We're also worrying about the cops or neighbors spotting us. Getting stiff and sore from not being able to move around, all this goes through your mind.

At the same time you are figuring how best to take the guy without the least bit of disturbance, the anticipation of knowing that within a few hours you could have plenty of bread if things go all right. At the same time you have to be

136

instantly ready to make your move at the right time; if you come at him too soon, he'll get back in the house or at least see your face; if you make your move too late, he'll be able to jump in the car and slam the door. And at all times he mustn't see your face. The thrill and excitement of the moment is there, like a boss high, but after so much time passes of just laying and waiting, the good feeling is replaced by a bummer. And unless you really concentrate, the boredom causes you to be less mentally alert. I never was the patient type and if I had my way, I'd go in the house and take whoever was there along with him.

Suddenly, spotlights light up the driveway. A car is pulling in. We tense, pistols ready. I feel no fear or worry; at least they're coming from the front and I have always felt capable of handling anything or anyone in front of me especially when I have a loaded automatic in my hand. Instantly I become alert, the good feelings of excitement alive in me. I nudge Louie and whisper to him to be sure he concentrates on the guy on the passenger side. I'll go after the driver. For sure we felt that something had gone wrong. Why else would Carmine have stayed in the house so long? And if these guys were supposed to meet with him, why did they take so long to come? He was not generally the man one kept waiting.

The situation was really tense. I started thinking that our fellows riding around in the cars were aware of this new happening, and that we just might be needing to get away in an awful hurry. As the car came to a stop, the front door of the house opened, and very casually some guy from the doorway said hello to those getting out of the car. They were taking suitcases out of the trunk of the car, and the guy from the house came out and helped carry them. Each of them had two suitcases. Me and Louie relaxed, obviously they had no idea we were there.

As the flow of adrenalin subsided in my body, my mind

told me this was something to be excited about. Something big was up. The whole situation meant this was a special thing. I couldn't put my finger on it, for sure, but even then, I felt we were missing the boat. I didn't wonder long what was in those suitcases. It had to be either heroin or money or both. The fact that T was there, the fact he was called there late unexpectedly, meant those six suitcases sure didn't contain clothes. Louie's mind couldn't handle this. He couldn't think that fast. And he couldn't do things unless they were thought out. I just felt that if I ripped those suitcases off, I'd really have a haul.

By this time all of them were in the house. I nudged Louie—get up and let's get back to the pickup spot. Veto picked us up almost immediately and I told him what happened and what I thought. We should wait and take those suitcases. It had to be a huge quantity of junk just smuggled in. I argued in vain. They had a dozen excuses why we couldn't do it. I told them there was no reason we shouldn't do it. If we did this we would never have to worry again about bread. There had to be heroin in those bags, I argued. I'm sure they knew it too, but they were just too scared. As time went by, and I had more dealings with them, I found out this was the case. They were short of heart. They wouldn't take any chances. And that was why they cut me into their deals. They knew I'd be the one to take all the chances.

By this time, we were well out of the neighborhood and on our way to the turnpike. I felt completely disgusted and let down. We drove the rest of the way back to the city in silence. I stopped off at an after-hours joint and downed about four or five shots of scotch in a matter of minutes. By the time I got home, my woman was getting up for work. This was the part I hated most. She didn't really know what I was up to, and I answered all her questions with lies. I didn't

138

enjoy lying to her, though I did so constantly. It was really hurting her, my being out all night every night. On the one hand, I wanted to stay home with her, but it was as if something compelled me to go out and do my thing. And it killed me when she would start crying. Many times she said she would support me if only I would stay home and be with her. I was a man with two personalities, and have been plagued with this makeup for years. I would be seriously torn up inside from the way I treated her, yet I would continue to do so. She was a very beautiful girl, and had lots of dates and fun when I met her. With me she was alone all the time, and I seldom took her out, though I went out with plenty of other girls. Usually, I had arranged my day in a manner where I wouldn't have to face her. I'd be sleeping when she got up for work, and I'd be sure to be out of the house by the time she got home from work. There was something inside me that I have never been able to figure out.

So now here it was, a week or so later, and T had found out that Carmine was going to be home early tonight, because his wife and kid were going down to Florida for a week. As soon as he took care of business tonight, he was heading straight home. This would be sometime about 10 or 11. We had decided to make sure that he was definitely heading home, then the car with me and Louie would get to his house first, drop us off, and we would wait in the bushes for him. Meanwhile the second car would stay well back behind Carmine's. During the last few days we were out practically every night, tracking him and losing him or not being able to get him in a safe manner. I had made up my mind, I was taking him tonight, no matter what.

Waiting for Mary to show, I felt like a new man. All the disgust and aggravation of the past weeks disappeared. I knew it would be over tonight. I lay there getting more sexually excited, yet it seemed even more than that. It was mental and physical. I had made it with Mary a few times; she wasn't that good in bed, but she really dug me, especially in bed. Her husband was a blank. The buzzer rang and I let her in.

I got dressed about seven that night. I dressed slowly and carefully, as I always did. I put the 9 mm. automatic in my belt feeling very sure of myself and powerful. Gone were all the bad moments of the last few weeks, even my life for that matter. I felt invincible; there was no one that could stop me, and I feared no one. I had an edge on them, simply because I wasn't afraid to die. I truly felt capable of dealing with anything or anyone. I drove over to the meeting place, thinking that given the slightest chance I was taking this guy tonight, whether or not the others agreed. I wasn't to be put off again. If Carmine showed like he was supposed to, I wasn't waiting. The others would have to go along with me, or else I'd go through the whole deal myself.

We met in an out-of-the-way place and discussed the plans. Me and Louie would hide in the shrubbery around the driveway, and when Carmine got out of the car we would step up to him, from behind, put the gun in his back, and slap on the dark, taped glasses, put him back in his car, drive to a prearranged spot, switch him to one of our cars, and drive straight to the motel. The room we had at the motel was naturally at the rear, so no one had to see him going in.

We got the call from T that Carmine was at a certain club. We got into our cars, me and Louie in one car, Veto in one and Richie in another. We drove downtown, got out of the cars, and sure enough we spotted Carmine's car down the block. We decided it would be best if Louie drove one car up to Connecticut and parked it at a convenient place in case things went wrong and one of us had to make a break for it, at least we would have a car to go to. We would wait for Carmine to come out and head home. Once he did Veto

140

would leapfrog with Richie, keeping an eye on Carmine's car, then right before he got off the turnpike Veto, with me in his car, would go ahead and pick up Louie at a certain place. Veto would drive us to Carmine's house and drop us off, and he'd go on to a spot that we had decided would be the best waiting spot for him. Richie would stay well back of Carmine's car and by the time he passed the driveway, we should already be in the process of taking Carmine. He'd keep going by slowly, and if he didn't hear any shots he'd know things went smoothly and that we had Carmine. He would drive by Veto's car at a normal speed which would tell Veto to expect us, that things went okay.

So Louie went on ahead. We had no idea, as we never did, just how long Carmine would stay in the club, and whether or not he would go right home or go to another club. With these people, things were always changing. I didn't like the fact we had to kind of hang out on the street, and each of us with guns on us. Naturally we spread out, but we had to remain somewhat near our cars. As always the time really dragged by. It seemed like hours and hours, when actually it was just about one hour when Veto saw him come out. He signaled to me and Richie. The tension was mounting in us, because we were praying he'd go home and nothing would come up, unexpected. The expectancy filled each of us. We followed him up Third Avenue, and I knew he wasn't going right home; he would have got on the East River Drive. He was heading for a club on Pleasant Avenue. Parking on that block, for us, would be a hell of a problem, so we had to chance parking three blocks down. We had to sit and wait again, hoping not for long.

We were in luck tonight. Sure enough he came out in twenty minutes or so. Now if he'd just go home like a good husband should. His car was easy to spot, being a brand new Cadillac. He got on the Drive and headed north. This was it.

He was going home. No hassle following him. Plenty of cars were on the road, he couldn't spot us. Just as Veto and I decided to pull ahead of him at the first chance, Carmine turned off at the Bronx exit. What the hell was this? We were lucky we hadn't already pulled ahead of him. For sure Veto and I would have lost him, and blown the whole deal. We got off behind him, thinking furiously where he was going. As we went up Bruckner Boulevard we tried to speculate. There were several places he might be heading. Most of them were known to us. We followed him up to a mob-hangout in the upper Bronx. He doubleparked, with his parking lights on. Relieved that he wasn't staying long—otherwise he would have parked in the lot across the street—we parked down the block. Five minutes later he came out, with another guy. What now? We could only guess, and that didn't do much good. Veto couldn't be sure, but he thought he knew the guy —one of the guys that hang around available for most anything. We went up Pelham Parkway and over to the New England Thruway. Carmine was going home. With this guy.

Right away Veto thought we should signal Richie and see if we should still go through with it. I told him, what the fuck, was he going to let one punk fuck us out of this whole deal? I assured him this presented no problem. Veto argued that perhaps Carmine was suspicious and that's why he was bringing this guy as a bodyguard. I insisted so what, we could handle this guy, and if worse came to worse, so what if he got hurt, as long as Carmine didn't. I told him me and Louie would wait as planned and if they got out of the car in a normal manner we would take them. But if they got out in a suspicious way, I'd tell Louie to cool it and as soon as they went in the house, me and Louie would leave. I convinced him of this, so he agreed. Fat chance of my cooling it. Unless he got out of that car with his gun cocked and aimed at us, I wasn't cooling anything.

We leapfrogged up as planned, and before we got near the turnoff, we sped ahead. Soon we reached the spot where Louie was waiting, picked him up, and drove past Carmine's house. Veto told Louie what had happened and that if things didn't look right to let it go. Louie agreed, but I knew that if I made the move Louie would have to back me up. We got out of the car a little past Carmine's house, and easily got into the bushes. We were both in the bushes by the driver's side. These were the closest to where the car had to park. In fact, the car would be about five or six feet away, no more.

This was great. Once we put the gun on Carmine, the goon wouldn't dare do anything for fear of Carmine. I felt good, knowing that for once we wouldn't have to wait indefinitely, and still not know anything. This time I knew Carmine would be coming in less than ten minutes. We both had our guns out, and I released the safety on mine. It felt good in my hand. I was on top again. I put the comic glasses with the false nose and moustache on. In the dark these would be enough to conceal my features. Louie did the same. Just at this time, we could see spotlights from a car slowing up, and then turning into the driveway. Now if he would just pull all the way up in the driveway, it would be perfect. He did, and I knew things were going to be okay. No stopping now.

We crouched down real low, we were even below the window level of the door. He was getting out very nonchalantly, not letting the goon get out first, which he would have if he suspected anything specific. As he slammed the door, his back was to us completely. We both rose up and stuck the guns in his back. I immediately pointed mine at the goon, and told them both in a very quiet, but authoritative tone, no one would get hurt, we just wanted their money. I said this so they would think that's all there was going to be. Otherwise, they might have thought it was a rubout, and certainly they wouldn't have given up easily if they thought that. They told us no hassle, just take the money, and for us not to get nervous with the guns. I told the goon to come around to this side of the car. I made them both lean up against the car, and acted just like all I wanted was their money. As the goon settled against the car, I smashed him in the head, and knocked him cold. Carmine got nervous and panicky. I grabbed him quick and told him not to make a sound. He wouldn't get hurt if he cooled it. Louie slapped the glasses on him, while I held the gun right to his head, just so he would know we were for real. I assured him we would kill him without hesitation if he made a sound. Louie got behind the wheel, and I handed him the keys. I had seen which pocket he had put them in. I pushed him into the back seat and followed him in. We backed out and drove away. This whole scene was executed in almost complete silence, and didn't take two or three minutes.

In the back of the car, I quickly blindfolded him more permanently, and soon we pulled alongside Veto. We hustled Carmine into the car, Richie picked up Louie and drove him to the car we had stashed. Since everything went along smoothly, there was no worry and no sense in leaving the car there to be picked up another time. Meanwhile, I put cuffs on Carmine and we headed back to New York. Again I made sure he couldn't see anything through the glasses. Veto had kept his head averted when we got Carmine into his car, and had on a wide-brimmed hat down over the back of his head. I told Carmine that if he caused any trouble at the tollbooths I wouldn't hesitate to kill him. He believed me, that's for sure. These people seldom give any trouble anyway. They would far rather give up the money than get hurt. They have so much money, they never worry about that. But they damn sure don't want to die.

We made it back to New York without any trouble, and it was easy as pie getting him into the motel room. Before putting on the lights, I removed the glasses from him and wrapped a cloth blindfold carefully around his eyes. As you can see the emphasis was on not getting seen by him. I pushed him onto the bed, on his stomach. Me and Veto would stay with him, while Richie made the phone call. We told Carmine what we wanted, and that if he didn't give us a number of who would cough up the money for him, we'd just as soon leave him there dead. Either we got the bread, or he would be dead; we made this point clear. We already knew several of his people, but we wanted to get the right number from him and the sure time to call. We didn't want to waste time finding out the right numbers. Richie left to make the calls. I wanted to go with him, but didn't push the point. Louie called and said he was heading home. This meant he was coming to the motel.

I just didn't like the whole phone business left in Richie's hands. I only had confidence in myself. About an hour later, he called and asked to meet Veto at a diner nearby. I insisted on going also. Louie could handle Carmine. When we got to the diner and sat over some coffee, Richie said they claimed they couldn't come up with a hundred grand that quick. They wanted to settle for 50 grand. Richie told them no good, and emphasized the point we would kill him. We had them over one barrel because we had Carmine, but they knew they had us also, because killing Carmine wouldn't get us a damn dime. So it was a bargaining session. Richie and Veto assured me this happened all the time. We agreed to settle for 75 grand, and I convinced Richie I should do the calling. Reluctantly he agreed.

I got the guy on the phone and told him very positively, that we would take 75 grand and not a dime less. I wasn't going to hassle with him. Take it or leave it. If I had to kill Carmine, I would, I didn't care, and then the next guy I kidnapped, they would know I meant business and they would damn sure get up all the bread. Besides, I told him, I knew him well and I'd come looking for him, and eventually I would catch him in a spot to kill him. I told him I had hand grenades and his bodyguards couldn't stop them. I also assured him I didn't care if I happened to kill his kids. This shook him up, because there is sort of a code not to hurt the family if you are after the mob guy. He quickly dug he was dealing with a nut, and after telling me what would happen when they caught me, he agreed to the 75 grand. I told him where he should drive, alone, along a straight stretch of road, where there was little if any traffic. He would see a car parked on the road, he should pull alongside just long enough to throw the bag in the car. He had to be sure there were no other cars on the road, and if so to double back. We knew there wouldn't be any funny stuff. They wanted Carmine alive. Of course there was always the danger of kidnapping some wheel that the mob didn't want back. But it was up to us to be sure that this didn't happen.

I went back to the motel, and Richie and Veto each drove a car out to the spot. Veto parked his and got into Richie's. They parked at a spot where they couldn't be seen and yet had a view of the road. They got there early just to be sure. Everything went fine, and they got the bread. They called us and we hustled Carmine back into the car. It was only about four o'clock, so it was still dark out enough. We took the cuffs off Carmine and I replaced them with some tape, just to slow him up a bit when we threw him out. We had to get rid of him quick, because it was getting light soon. I had really wished it was darker out. This could be risky. We drove to a small quiet street in the west Bronx. I pushed him out and we took off.

I breathed a sigh of relief. It was over. Now the money. Seventy-five grand, wow, the thought of this made me tell Louie to hurry. For a moment I thought of Richie and Veto

146

crossing me. When I offhandedly remarked to Louie the possibility of this he assured me not to worry about that. He knew them a long time. I realized I knew where each of them lived, along with their families. Plus Richie owned a nice house with swimming pool and all. He wasn't about to pack up that quickly even if he wanted to. He also had to realize that I could easily phone in an anonymous tip to the mob and give his name along with Veto's. So I felt assured they'd be there with the dough. I did feel uneasy, though, so when I walked into the pad we rented I had my hand on my gun and was very watchful. After all, I didn't really know these cats.

They had already split up the dough, and handed me a stack. They were all used bills naturally, and as I flipped through it I saw hundreds and fifties and twenties. I would have liked to have seen the whole 75 grand to see how fat a pile it made. After expenses and a full cut for the tipster, we each had a little more than 14 grand. That sure was a long way from 75 grand. Immediately, the thought went through my mind I could have it all, but I'd have to really take a chance. Too big a chance. I couldn't risk gunfire, and the situation wasn't right. So I forgot it. Richie dropped me off where my car had been parked and I drove home, feeling relieved it was all over. I woke up my girl, and before she got over being surprised at my being home, I started making love to her.

13

I awoke early the next day, still filled with the excitement of the night before. I got up and recounted the money and spread it over the bed. I caressed my gun, reveling in the power of it. It was a beautiful gun, a 9 mm. automatic which held nine bullets in the clip and one in the chamber. Who could stop me? Who was better than I? I got dressed, put the money in my two front pockets, and the gun in my belt. I knew just what I was going to buy.

I went immediately to the new car dealer, where I had seen this beautiful Thunderbird. As I was looking at the cars, a salesman came up and started giving me a sales talk. I told him shut up and how long would it take for delivery of a T-Bird. At the same time, I handed him a $50 bill. He told me he would rush it and it would take at the most ten days to two weeks. I counted out the money, watching his eyes bulge. A little under 7 grand. Then I went and bought some clothes: Italian silk suits and slacks, along with a mohair top-coat. Then I went around the neighborhood and paid off all my debts.

The money didn't last long, what with going to the trotters each night and nightclubbing afterwards. I had been spending anywhere from one to two hundred dollars each night at the clubs. I guess you could call it a good life, and when I wasn't searching into myself, I enjoyed it. But there were times I felt very frustrated. Everything seemed so plastic: the bars, the guys, and the girls. As long as you had money to spend, or as long as people thought you were into something, they'd glad-hand you and crowd around. But it wasn't for real. Inside I knew this, but I concentrated on keeping my thoughts only on the surface and living each moment without a thought.

I started getting heavy into coke then. I had met and made friends with this guy, Scotty, who was the biggest coke supplier to black Harlem at that time. Every night he would go through several hundred dollars of coke, with what he used himself and what he gave to those who were drinking with him. I was fucking this socialite, who was the girl friend of a fairly famous singer at the time. Through her, I fixed Scotty up with one of her friends, a real classy beauty. Shit, the parties we had. Stoned out of our minds and fucking all day.

One night I met Jackie, who had been up in the joint with me. He had always been a heavy card player, and he told me he was running bad, losing his shirt at some card game in Jersey. He was deep in hock to the shylocks and he was looking for a way to make some bread. I started asking him about the card game and who was running it. Of course some rackets were, but I didn't recognize their names. He gave me a layout of the place, and the password that would get me in. I told him I would cut him in for a share if he drove the car. I didn't know Jersey and I would need some one who did. Besides, if he was in on the stickup, I knew he wouldn't be tempted to rat me out for the reward.

149

He was kind of shook-up at first. He had been brought up to believe that no one crossed the Mafia and lived. I told him, they weren't God, and if no one knew who did it, who could they come looking for? Besides, I explained, I was doing all the dirty work. I would be taking the risk by going inside, while he would be out in the car. Finally, he agreed.

I called up this black guy whom I knew upstate. He was a crazy bastard with a lot of balls. He was well respected in prison by both the blacks and the whites. While he was big and strong and could probably beat most guys with his hands, he preferred piping them. I had seen him a few times at the parole officer's office, and he had told me he was looking to make a score. I made a meet with him and told him of the plan.

He agreed immediately, but expressed his doubts of Jackie not panicking in case of shooting. I was a little leery of that myself. If we had to shoot our way out, Jackie just might pull out without us. The best thing to do, I said, is to have another car parked in front with the keys in the ignition. This way if Jackie split, we could jump in the other car and get away. Ned said okay, he dug that. The three of us got together and it was decided we would do it the following Monday. Jackie figured there should be about 50 grand in the game. Immediately, the familiar, crazy exhilarating feeling came over me. The risk of what I was doing gave me the only thrill worth living for.

Finally, Monday came. We met in New York, Jackie in one stolen car, Ned in another, and I in my year-old Le Mans. We drove out to Jackie's house in Jersey where I would leave my car. I gave Jackie a 12-gauge shotgun, and told him if anybody came out of that door after us, just blow them away. Chances are, he wouldn't have to use it, but not to hesitate if push came to shove. I gave Ned a sawed-off shotgun, and went over the plan with him. I told him not to hurt anybody

150

unless it was absolutely necessary. I was aware of his penchant for hurting people.

Ned and I drove to the game and pulled up a bit down the block. Jackie was to wait a block away and then when he saw us go in he was to pull up in front of the place. My hands were sweating as the excitement swept over me. There were double doors and Ned was to wait outside the outer door while I went in and gave the signal on the inner door. I went in and gave the knock Jackie told me to use. The peephole opened and I saw an eye. I said Leo was a friend of mine and he told me it was okay for me to come. I heard a grunt and the bolts sliding back.

As the door opened I pushed through with my automatic in my hand. Immediately Ned was behind me. We slammed the door shut. By now everyone was looking up and I yelled to them, "The first motherfucker that moves one inch gets blown away." Ned had moved alongside and everyone there was aware of the damage that shotgun could do. There were about 15 guys in the place. I had them all line up against the wall. We had plenty of time. If anyone came knocking at the door, we would simply let them in. Everything was cool.

I told them to all be sure to give me all the money in their pockets. If I found one of them holding out, he'd be a sorry motherfucker. Each of them handed me their money. I put it in the paper bag, along with the bread from the table. Then I made them all strip, buck naked. I kicked all their clothes in a corner. As we were leaving I told them if one of them showed his face at the door he would get a shotgun blast. Just as we were leaving, one of them said, "You know what's going to happen when we find you." Ned, furious at being threatened, called him a guinea motherfucker, and smashed him in the face with the butt of the shotgun. Immediately blood spurted from his face and he screamed in pain. Ned went over to kick him and I told him to cool it.

151

We went out, walked to the car and got in. Jackie was full of questions as he drove away. It was obvious he was scared. I told him everything went cool and there was nothing for him to worry about. We made it to his house, where we split up a little over 20 grand. Ned was laughing and talking excitedly about "Did you see that motherfucker's face when I bashed him?" I didn't particularly dig him hitting that guy. I am not one for hurting somebody unless provoked. Well, it was over with, and I didn't figure to see Ned again for a while. More than likely, I wouldn't ever have to use him again.

I gathered up the guns, warned Jackie and Ned of the consequences if they even mentioned this to their friends, got in my car and headed back to the city. Jackie was to drive Ned to the bus terminal and ditch the car. Feeling the power inside me, I speeded back to New York. Fortunately, I wasn't stopped by the Jersey troopers. I dropped the guns off at my house, went back downtown and met the fellows for a night full of drinking.

I guess the way it sounds here is that I was a master thief and everything always went smoothly and the money was easy to come by. To be truthful, for every one that went okay, several were fucked up and we wound up with nothing but thin air.

I remember the time we were taking off this numbers guy. We had been trailing him for a couple weeks now, and always at the last minute, something went wrong. Finally, one night we got the call he was in his club. We knew where he was going when he left his club—right to Pleasant Avenue.

We got ourselves ready about a block from his club, which was on Third Avenue. Veto and Richie would sit in their car a half a block back. Me and Louie stationed ourselves as close to the club as we could without being too conspicuous. The numbers guy's car was double-parked in front. We would approach him as soon as he was getting into his car. Lots of people were passing by in the street, but we weren't worried about them. If things went as planned they wouldn't even know something was happening. Me and Louie planned to get into the car with him and drive away with Richie and Veto following. We would drive him to the west side where we had a car stashed. We would put him into the other car, blindfold him and take him to the motel room we were paying each night for.

It was about two in the morning, and it wasn't too easy standing around looking cool. I was thinking some cop might come up and decide to frisk me. "Come on you bastard, leave that fucking club," I said to myself. I had taken my eyes off the club for just a minute and sure enough the bastard had come out. I walked quickly to the driver's side and just as I got there he closed the door. He had the type of car where you can lock all the doors from the driver's side. I flashed this badge at him and said, "Treasury agent, open up." The badge was authentic looking.

Meanwhile Louie was on the other side of the car. The guy seemed like he was going to open the door; then he hesitated and said "What's it about?" I told him just open up and we'll discuss it. That's when he got scared. The trouble with taking these guys off is that the first thing that comes to their heads is they're going to get knocked off, that some mob guy they rubbed wrong hired some killers to take care of them. I'm sure that's what this guy believed. I pulled out my gun and told him if he didn't open the door I'd blow his head off. I pointed the gun right at him. The fool ducks down in the seat, as if he could avoid getting shot that way. I start banging on the window with the butt of my gun, but these fucking windows ain't about to break. In desperation the guy starts the car up and pulls away, leaving me in the street looking like an idiot.

153

Veto and Richie pull up, and me and Louie jump in. They say forget about it, we blew it, but I insist fuck that shit. "We know where he is going, let's get there before him." But they say no. "God damn these scared motherfuckers." I'm angry with frustration and disappointment. We could have got maybe 75 grand for this guy. Just one more step and I would have been at the door before he even got behind the wheel. Shit! Suddenly, up ahead we see his car stopped. Alongside is a motorscooter cop giving him a ticket, probably for speeding. I tell the guys, come on man, we can still get him now. We'll be there before him. But they ain't going for it. We pull up on Pleasant Avenue just to see what happens. A few minutes later, the guy pulls up, jumps out of his car, and runs up the stoop. He was one scared motherfucker. And I was one angry motherfucker.

Another incident was even more frustrating. Our tipster informs us that this guy Manny, a rackets boss, keeps over 100 grand in his house. He's married, lives out in a high-class section of Long Island, and has two big sons who also live out on the Island, but not with him. He also spends the night occasionally with a girl friend who also lives on the Island. We get the guy's address along with his girl friend's, from the tipster and we drive by the guy's house to look it over.

There's bushes close to the front door, which will make a perfect hiding place. Then when he gets out of his car and walks to the door, me and Louie can come up behind him and walk in the front door with him. We plan to tie him up and make him tell us where the money is stashed. It seemed an easy touch. Just him and his wife in the house. At night it is a very dark area with plenty of trees and bushes all around, and he generally leaves his restaurant around two in the morning.

Again our problem is to hang around the area of his

restaurant inconspicuously. This isn't so easy to do, as it is a very high-class neighborhood and patrolling cops are liable to wonder why a guy is hanging around the streets. Me and Veto are on the sidewalk, separated of course. It's a scary thing, knowing a cop can come up to you at any minute and you got a gun on you. We have a car parked down the block so we can follow him once he leaves. Louie and Richie are in a corner bar where they can watch us. When they see us head for our car, they will get in theirs and we will take turns following him.

It's winter time and cold out. So many nights when things looked liked they'd work out, he'd come out with his sons. Of course we couldn't do anything with them with him. We couldn't just wait for him out by his house for two reasons. One, since we never knew for sure just what time he'd head home, it was too risky hanging around his neighborhood; besides, we never knew if he was going home or to his girl friend's house. So we were forced to follow him from the city out to the Island. Many nights we froze our asses off waiting for him to come out, and he would be with his sons.

Finally, one night, we see his two sons leave early. This is it, we tell ourselves. If he goes to his girl's house, we'll intercept him there and take him to his own house. So we wait and we wait, and the wind is blowing stronger, and we freeze. Finally, the lights go dim; he's closing up. Already, I see Richie and Louie heading for their car. As we see him coming out the door, Veto and I nonchalantly walk to our car. He pulls out, we pull out, followed by Richard and Louie, through the streets heading for the Midtown Tunnel. We daren't lose him, yet we can't risk him spotting us. In our own paranoia of being followed, we assume everyone else is. Out along the expressway we follow, the tension and thrill mounting up inside me. Shit, I tell myself, ain't no way we're going to miss tonight. He pulls off an exit. The bastard is going to his girl's house which makes it a bit harder. I knew things couldn't go smooth.

Since we now know where he's going we don't have to follow him any longer. We pull ahead of him and head to his girl's house. There, Veto drops me off, and shortly after Richie drops Louie off. There is a covering of snow on the ground and as we walk to some bushes our footprints leave a telltale sign. He won't even notice them I tell myself, and even if he does, there's no way he can tell they weren't made this afternoon. So me and Louie wait, in the snow, freezing, worrying if some cop's car won't see the prints and investigate.

It's freezing out, but we can't move around. We have to remain perfectly still. Time goes by—10 minutes—where the hell is he? A half hour, what the fuck is happening? Did he stop for coffee? This is ridiculous.

We see the lights of a car approaching. We huddle deeper behind the bushes. The car is moving slowly. Cops, I tell Louie. Oh shit, man, I ain't going to get busted like this. I start looking for a place to run. We don't even know the area, and if we run and Veto or Richie don't find us how will we ever get out of this section. Once the cops see us running, they'll have every prowl car in the neighborhood out. All these thoughts going through my head, I grip my gun tighter, and hold my breath. The cops are passing the house now. We're just 20 feet from them. Are the bushes thick enough? I don't even think I can run. I'm too frozen. The car passes. We release our breaths.

We wait for Veto to come by as planned and we head out to the street to meet him. An hour has gone by and that Manny ain't showed up. Something is wrong, that's obvious. We get in the car, pass by Richie in his car and tell him we are going back to the city. So we all head home. We stop for coffee, and after several cups of steaming coffee, my body just barely begins to thaw out. We can't imagine what went wrong. The next night, I get the word from Richie. We were waiting at the wrong house. The girl friend lived in another section. We had the address screwed up. What fucking idiots. Back to following the motherfucker again.

Again the whole routine. After waiting for hours the bastard comes out with his sons. We decide it's really not safe to hang around every night. Someone is sure to spot us. So we go every other night. And with our luck, the nights we go, he's either not there, or he's with his sons. Then one night he comes out with his sons. Disappointed again, but no, we see them saying good night to him and they get into one car and he goes to another. This is it, I tell myself. Nothing can go wrong tonight. I start thinking of my end of 100 grand. Even further I start thinking of how I can wind up with all the money. I could shoot these motherfuckers, but that would make too much noise. Besides while no one could prove anything, there would be a lot of heat on me, unless I got the tipster too.

We follow him out along the expressway again. He passes the exit where his girl friend lives. My heart pumps quicker. He's going home. About time. We pull up ahead of him keeping him in our rear-view mirror just to be sure. As we get off the exit in front of him, for a moment I worry whether he's getting off the exit too. He does! We speed up to get there before him. Louie and I get out around the corner and walk towards his house making sure no one is looking. We duck for the bushes.

We wait maybe five, ten minutes. Headlights are coming, and the car pulls into the driveway. As he is getting out of the car, the outside lights come on. The door opens and two women are standing in the door. I thought only his wife is supposed to be here. Fuck it. Just as he reaches the door, we step out of the bushes and push him inside, closing the door behind us. I show him my gun and tell them if they make a sound they're dead.

One woman is about 20 and the other about 60. His wife starts talking loudly and excitedly. I tell him to shut her up or else. He calms her down, and I head them to the back of the house. There's a bedroom there and I herd them into it. I make them lie down on the bed, face down. We blindfold them, after which Louie opens the door for Richie and Veto. Warning them to keep their faces down, we tie them up.

I ask Manny where the money is. He swears he doesn't have any in the house. I threaten him, he tells me about his heart and there are some pills in the drawer he has to take. We give them to him. His wife is struggling and I can see she is having trouble breathing. He tells me she has asthma. I loosen the gag from her mouth, telling her if she makes a sound I'll put it back on. Richie succeeds in getting the guy to tell where he has the money hidden. An envelope taped to the bottom of the bureau. We open it up, and it's obvious it's a long way from 100 grand. A bit more than four thousand is in the envelope. We go through the house and turn up maybe two thousand more.

I get really disgusted with this bastard. I put the gun to his head and eject the bullet in the chamber but sending one in from the clip. The sliding action and click terrifies him, but he still swears he has no more money. I go to the kitchen and get a knife, telling him if he doesn't tell I'm going to carve up his wife. He starts crying and swearing if he had more he would tell us. He's begging for mercy. I tell him there were plenty of people that begged him for mercy but he still had them killed. I'm convinced he doesn't have any more bread in the house. Another bum tip. Richie and Veto are going through the jewelry picking out the stuff that's worthwhile. I go to the icebox, and find some cold chicken and soda. We

158

pull out the phones and leave. I tell Richie he better have a good talk with the tipster.

I drive home feeling down. I know something is wrong with my life. I don't mean my conscience was bothering me, not in the least. I couldn't put my finger on it, but something was missing from my life. Part of me was a void. Part of me just wasn't alive. I had no feelings. I knew I was as superficial as everything I condemned. This wasn't the life for me, but what other life did I have? I had no friends, but did I really want any? What did I really know about myself? Ah, fuck it, I told myself. This is the only life for me. Too many things have happened for me to change. Besides, what else could I be or do?

I pushed these thoughts out of my mind, and quickly resumed my cold, callous, uncaring being. Too many people had shit on me, and now it was my turn to shit on others. I got home and called up one of my girl friends. She came over and I made love to her savagely.

I was spending money as fast as I made it. Drinking, going to the trotters, which I knew nothing about, and playing cards. I hated but didn't know just who to hate. It's hard to hate in general. It's frustrating not knowing just who to direct your hate towards. I began getting very edgy. I began pushing my weight around. It took me a few weeks to settle down. During that period I had made a couple of enemies because of my attitude. Certain people were telling me to be cool otherwise there would be trouble for me, and I just told them to fuck off. I felt completely alone.

What helped me get over this down period was another kidnapping. We took this guy real easy as he was going into his house, and drove him to a motel. We called his brother and told him we wanted 50 grand. Finally we settled for 30 grand.

Just a few weeks later, we decided to kidnap the brother.

159

He lived in upstate New York and we had to wait in the bushes a few nights until he came home before dawn. The closest bushes were across the street from where he lived. We had to get him as soon as he got out of the car, otherwise he'd break for the house. Richie and Veto were parked down the street. As he pulled up in front of his house, me and Louie got ready to run across the street. He opened the car door and stepped out. Just as he did, I broke across the street gun in hand, yelling "Don't move, we're Federal agents." The bastard slipped back into the car and immediately starts backing the car up. Furious, I fired a shot through the window. By now he had the car in forward and he roared away. We ran to where Richie was parked and we got into the wind. They were angry at me for firing the shot, but didn't push the issue too much, knowing I had a bad temper. That bastard was smart. When he got out of the car, he had left the motor running until he saw everything was okay. That's why he was able to get moving so fast.

The tipster told us next day, we better be cool for a while. The rackets guys were really furious and they had put out a reward for the guys ripping them off. They would even give the reward and let go any one of the gang that was involved if he told who the others were. They were so shook up, that the top guys wouldn't even head home without a car full of bodyguards following. The heat was really on. Word reached me through my own friends in the rackets that if they caught the guys they would torture them first as a lesson before killing them.

I immediately became even more cautious. I moved the very next day. I didn't put myself in any position where I could be set up. I now carried my automatic in my topcoat pocket and kept my hand on it as I walked. There was no reason for me to suspect they were after me, but I wasn't taking any chances. It was exciting. The biggest thrill in life is risking your life, and my life was certainly on the line. I felt confident that no one could take me. I could handle whatever situation I was in.

During this period, I had some trouble from an unsuspected source. There were a bunch of would-be Mafia guys hanging out in a club uptown. I knew one of them well from prison. He was just getting started dealing heavy in heroin. We ran across each other every so often and we would buy each other drinks. He was always after me to get him a broad.

One night I told my girl to meet me up in their club. For some reason I couldn't get up there, so I called to tell her to take a cab and meet me someplace else. The guy that answered the phone first tried to say she wasn't there. Then he said she was busy eating. I told him bullshit, put her on the phone. She tells me they were all eating together and had invited her to sit down with them. When I told her to take a cab right away she said they insisted she finish eating with them. She wanted to leave but she was scared it would cause bad feelings. Who the fuck did they think they were?

I told her I would be right up. I jumped in my car angry as a bastard. Them motherfuckers thought they were tough playing the Mafia bit. I was sick of their acting like big shots. I stormed through the bar into the back where the tables were. I grabbed her hand and said she is going with me, and fuck what anybody says. This guy I know jumps up and tells me I should have more respect than to be talking that way. I told him fuck your respect and who the fuck do you think you were making her stay here. A couple of the guys started saying something and I cut them off saying if they wanted trouble I'd give them plenty of trouble. With that I left.

Later that night I get the word that they were going to teach me a lesson. I didn't give a fuck. I knew I was tougher than any one of those fucks. The fellows in the bar where I hung out knew all these guys so they had to remain in neutral.

About two weeks later, as I left the bar and walked to my car on the next block I spotted these two guys in a doorway near my car. Lately, I was suspicous of anybody I saw hanging out. I watched them knowing they could easily be just two people shooting the breeze. I had a strange feeling something just wasn't right. The closer I got the more shady these guys looked. I pulled my hand with the gun in it up out of my pocket just a bit. Just when I reached my car, I saw them take a step toward me. One of them said, "Hey, we want to talk with you." I pulled my gun out and seeing something in the hands of one of them, I fired. The noise was deafening. He fell to the ground and I heard the object he was holding bounce on the concrete. It was an iron pipe, with which they were going to work me over. The other guy was running like mad down the block. I got into my car and sped away.

I got home and called the bar. I got the story some guy got shot in the stomach down the block. No one knows who did it. The guy was supposed to be in a bad way, according to the cops. Anyway I found out his name. I called the hospital, claiming to be his brother and could I have a report on my brother's condition. They said his condition was poor but they believed the wound wasn't fatal.

I knew who had set this up. I called the bastard on the phone and told him if they tried some shit again, I would come directly for him. I promised him sooner or later I'd catch him in the right position and I'd blow his head off with a shotgun. He knew I was a crazy bastard and I would keep my word. I figured I had better give the air a chance to clear. I took a plane to Puerto Rico and checked into a hotel. The second day there, who do I run in to but Scotty. He had an entire suite upstairs and insisted I move in with him. I can

162

tell you, we had one hell of a ball. Plenty of girls, booze and coke. We did the casinos at night. I came back with him about 10 days later.

Back in the neighborhood, just about everyone knew by now I was the guy that shot that stud. Two of the cops we were paying off came into the bar. When they saw me they came over and told me I was a lucky guy. Fortunately the guy was alive and the trouble would just blow over, but if he had died there would have been a big hassle and I would have been brought in. I knew what they were fishing for so I gave them each $100.

Out on the streets word was still out that the rackets guys wanted the guys ripping them off. I was ever cautious because I couldn't know for sure if Richie, Veto or Louie would be scared enough to sell out. And I knew the fellows uptown I had fucked over would look to get me sooner or later. I wasn't worried; on the contrary, life was much more interesting to me. The thrill was always present.

I guess I always knew things would come to a head sooner or later, but I didn't give it much thought. Fuck it; live for today, the hell with tomorrow. I was living fast, and there were a lot of people afraid of me. This isn't cool, cause either they'll get you, or they'll get the cops to get you, which I found out firsthand.

14

I awoke from a troubled sleep and lay there trying to get myself together. My body was full of anxiety; it was a very strange feeling that comes over me once in a while. It's as if everything is vibrating inside, and causes me to be very restless. I gave up trying to go back to sleep. I dressed quietly so as not to wake my wife, and took the dog out for a walk. She was a beautiful trained shepherd and very protective.

As I walked, my head was filled with what had happened in the bar last night. Bob and John had told me they were going to kill Larry, and they wanted my help in setting him up. They had been trying for a week to find him with no success, so they figured he must be hiding out at his wife's place.

I didn't have to ask why they were going to knock him off. He had been shooting his mouth off for some time and was getting to be one big pain in the ass. I had threatened to shoot him myself. More than likely, the bastard was hiding out at his wife's. The creep had left her seven months ago, pregnant and alone. She was due to have her baby this month.

I thought of Lorraine, his wife. We had become very close friends. She was young, nineteen, and very attractive. She was a good girl, which seems to be a rarity nowdays. I had helped her out, giving her money for food and stuff. She was the one person I could really feel at ease with. What made it stranger was the fact I never made love to her though we slept together many times. I guess if I had tried I could have, but she had a special quality of goodness and niceness about her. I knew if we made love, it would put our relationship on a different level, and neither one of us wanted that. She was the one refuge I could escape to when I wanted to be my real self and completely relax. I guess I loved her very much in an undefined way.

She wasn't angry that Larry left her. She accepted it as just another unhappy happening in her already unhappy life. She had had a very rough time, being kicked around from home to home in her childhood. I was amazed at her ability not to be bitter. She still believed in the goodness of people. She was barely surviving on welfare and yet she had a quality of gentleness and love. I envied her strength. When I was with her, surrounded by her serenity, I actually felt I was in the presence of an angel.

Aside from my own personal problems with Larry, I hated him even more for having fucked Lorraine around.

I told Bob and John that it wouldn't be cool to go looking for Larry at his wife's. I made it clear that she was a personal friend of mine and I didn't want her involved in any way. They said all they wanted to do was to take him out of the house and leave him somewhere dead. They needed my help in getting into the house. I made it clear I wanted no part of it and I would take it personal if they went near Lorraine's house. All they had to do was wait and he would come out of hiding, and it would be an easy thing to get him then. They agreed and said that was the best thing, and we left it like that. I had a date with two girls so I split to pick them up.

As I walked the dog, I tried to think how Lorraine would take Larry's getting shot. Would it affect her having the baby? That motherfucker, even in his dying he'd fuck her around some more. I thought of taking her upstate somewhere, but I knew that wouldn't work, as she had already made arrangements with the hospital. I decided to go over to see her as soon as I dropped the dog off. Then I realized it was still too early; I'd go over later in the afternoon.

Returning to my house, I decided to have an egg cream at the candy store. As I ordered the egg cream, I glanced at the papers laying on the counter. "Three shot in apt." the headlines glared. My eyes traveled down the article and God my heart almost stopped. Lorraine was dead! They did it, the motherfuckers, they went over to her house to get Larry and shot Lorraine. Those dirty stinking rotten motherfuckers. I grabbed the paper, threw some money down and stumbled home. "No, there had to be a mistake," I told myself, but inside, I knew better. I was filled with love and hate. Love for Lorraine and hate for Bob and John.

I hurried upstairs to read the article. My wife was still sleeping as I sat on the bed to read. Larry and his friend had been shot in the kitchen and Lorraine was shot in the bedroom. I knew his friend. A very legitimate college-going kid. I could imagine what had happened. The killers went in to get Larry, and because his friend happened to be there they had to kill him too. And because Lorraine's body had been found between the bed and the bedroom door, she must have gotten up, after hearing the shots, and they killed her too for fear of being identified later. The paper stated she was rushed to the hospital and an attempt was made to save the baby but it was too late. I sat there, kind of in a daze. I felt

166

as if the only good thing in my life was gone. My last touch with innocent love and decency. I told myself I would avenge her death and kill Bob and John. Those bastards, I told them to leave her alone. I'd get them I swore.

Suddenly there was a loud pounding at the door. "Open up, this is the police." Shit, I hadn't even taken the time to realize I would be a prime suspect. The local cops knew I knew Larry and at one time he had hung out in our bar. The door crashed open and the room was filled with cops and plainclothesmen all with guns in their hands. My wife awoke in shock seeing all those guns pointed at us. I had to grab my dog and hold her and one of the cops said if that dog moves I'll put a bullet in him. The cops searched me and when they saw there was to be no trouble they put their guns away. They wanted to talk to me at the station. They assured me that was all they wanted to do. They were bringing in the people that knew Larry and all they wanted to do was to question them.

I asked them, then why all the guns, and one of them answered, "Well, we've been hearing some stories about you." Some of the cops in the crowd knew me; in fact, three or four of them I had paid off at various times. I told them I knew nothing about what happened last night other than what I read in the paper. I asked them if they had a warrant for my arrest. I was told I was not under arrest, all they wanted to do was talk. When I insisted on calling my lawyer, they told me not to bother him, they would only keep me about an hour. I called him anyway. I really wasn't worried cause I knew I was innocent, and besides I had a good alibi for last night. My main concern was the two guns I had hidden in the house. Before they took me out, I asked if I could speak with my wife. I explained she was pregnant and I wanted to calm her down and assure her I would be okay. They agreed, and I hurriedly whispered to her to get rid of

167

the guns in the closet. I suspected correctly they would be back to search as soon as they got a warrant.

There was something strange about this whole thing. They came crashing in with guns drawn, then they put them away. They didn't handcuff me, they didn't search (I've yet to meet a cop that didn't search just because he lacked a warrant), they were talking nice to me, and they let me talk to my wife in a private room. And how the fuck did they find out where I lived in the first place? At the very most only three people knew where I lived; two of them were the killers, and the other lived out in Jersey. None of them were in a position to give the police any information. Still, I wasn't worried. I could prove where I was last night.

At the station house, I insisted I knew nothing about the murders. I told them to check with the girls I was with last night and even some of the bars we had gone to; I knew the bartenders and they would verify my whereabouts.

The police station was crowded with cops. There was also a couple of guys I knew from the neighborhood, but we were kept separated. I was then brought into another room and questioned by a single detective. There was a one-way glass in the wall and I knew they were bringing people into the adjoining room so they could look through the glass at me for possible identification. (A funny side note here is that while no one made a possible identification on me, the detective was picked out by two people as the man that stuck them up.) By now I had been in the station house several hours. I heard a cop and a woman on the other side of the one-way glass arguing. The cop was saying, "Listen, lady, you don't have to be afraid of him. He's not getting out, he just killed three people. Go ahead and identify him. The lady was insisting I was not the guy that stuck her up." I later found out a supermarket she was working in had been stuck up by Larry, and the cops were trying to pin it on me. The lady was getting bugged by the cop pressuring her and finally she yelled, "That's not him, God damn it, and you can't make me say it is."

I suddenly started thinking I was in big trouble. These cops were really trying to pin something on me. Someone from the neighborhood that knew me well was feeding the cops a lot of information. They knew I had threatened Larry and told him I was going to blow his head off. The cops also knew I had just come back from down south where I had bought four guns. It dawned on me there were quite a few people that didn't want me back out on the streets and they just might be trying to set me up on this murder rap.

The captain of homicide came in and told me I might just as well tell them everything. "We know you were one of the killers. Even your alibi doesn't stand up. We checked with the bars and the two girls, and there was a period where you were gone for a half hour—just long enough to get to Larry's house and back." I didn't know if this was just some game he was trying or if he really got the girls into saying I had been gone for that long. Shit, the only time I left the girls was to make a phone call and that couldn't have been more than five or ten minutes at the most.

My wife had come over to the precinct and they let me talk to her for a few minutes. She told me the cops told her I had killed a nine-months-pregnant girl, or I was at least involved in it. That really shook her up, especially her being pregnant too. I assured her I knew nothing about it. She knew I was capable of doing a lot of things, but definitely not something like this.

After she left, a detective came over to me and asked me if either me or my wife knew anyone that drove a black Buick. I replied no, why? Then offhandedly he says, well two guys in a black Buick were following your wife. "If you care at all about your wife, you better tell us what you know cause those two guys both looked like hoods." I got a little panicky because this fucking cop just might be telling the truth, or he just might be bullshitting to shake me up a little. I didn't put it past Bobby and John, or one of their friends to terrorize my wife so as to be sure I kept my mouth shut. I began putting the threads together. Under ordinary conditions they both knew I would never open up, so why are they worrying now. Of course, if I found out they were setting up a frame they could figure, I just might get mad enough to open up to save myself.

A few minutes later the cops came in with this bookie I had stuck up a few weeks ago. Aside from taking his money I also took his payoff book and there were quite a few cops' and detectives' names in it. He tells the two cops I am the guy that stuck him up. I'm wondering what the fuck is he doing here; he can't afford to testify against me. The two cops are screaming at me now. "Okay you bastard, we got you now. You'll never see the streets again."

"I got to keep my head," I tell myself. "There's so much shit coming down, I got to stay cool. This guy can't really go to court. This has to be just a scare, besides, I got the book." The book, that's the answer. And these cops' names must be in that book, else they would never have got him to come here. And one name I remembered good: Lou; he's that big heavy, mean bastard. His name is all over that book. So I tell the cops I want to talk to Lou, he's a detective. They knew who I meant all right. They had him in there in two minutes.

Before he has a chance to open his mouth, I tell him, "Okay Lou, they got this fuck to identify me and they're threatening to go to court with this. Yeah, I ripped him off, and I still got the book. And if you charge me with this, I'll have that book put in the District Attorney's hands, and this whole precinct will be in trouble. A lot of people ain't going to like that.

170

"And listen, screaming at me ain't going to do no good, cause I'm a crazy motherfucker and I'd just as soon blow this whole thing out in the open, right here and now."

"Tell us where the book is and we'll forget about the robbery."

"Like hell," I tell him. "Without that book I'm dead. I ain't robbed anybody legitimate, so you can't get me for that. The only people you can get to identify me is some creep like this and that book is my protection."

It's a stalemate and they realize it, so they take the bookie out. Then Lou comes back in and tells me I am up-tight on the murder rap, and I better tell what I know and protect myself. He says there's a lot of people convincing the cops I was one of the killers, and if I don't protect myself, I am going to get hung. I insist I know nothing. "Okay, it's your ass," he says.

The next thing I know I'm getting booked for robbery of a supermarket. The irony of it is that there are cops that know I didn't do it but of course they're keeping their mouths shut. They couldn't get enough to hold me for the murders, so they put this shit on me to keep me in custody.

I didn't believe they could keep me very long in jail. I knew I didn't commit the crime and I felt I would get cut loose as soon as I had a hearing. They couldn't have any witnesses against me unless they got one to lie. My wife was all that kept me from exploding. She came to visit me every chance allowed. I sent her up to the supermarket I was charged with robbing to find out what was going on. The guy up there swore he never said I was the guy. I repeated this to my lawyer and told him to demand a hearing. But the D.A. was really trying to fuck me around. He kept stalling and had the case put before one of the judges. When I applied for bail he showed the judge the photos taken of the three people killed, and told the judge I was involved in it and it was just a matter of time till they got the evidence.

Meantime the cops were terrorizing my wife. They were making anonymous calls to her and saying she was going to be killed and just because she was pregnant didn't mean a damn thing. They followed her constantly and she was feeling the strain. She didn't know if it was the cops or gangsters. I was going crazy being helpless inside. She was getting big and the baby was due pretty soon. The D.A. kept telling me all the things I was doing, who I had robbed and whose games I had stuck up. Someone was feeding the information to him. It was obvious by now there were people that didn't want me out because of fear of what I might do.

One morning the captain stops by my cell and very matter-of-factly tells me my wife had the baby and it died but my wife was all right. I had been counting on having that baby. I felt so damn disgusted with myself, my life, with everything. Nothing had ever worked out with my life. When I saw my wife again she was very depressed and on the verge of hysteria. I kept arguing with my lawyer to get my case called.

Meanwhile they had caught two of the guys that did the murders and the cops were trying to prove I was the third guy. The people that were paying these cops off were convincing the cops I was the guy. I had told my wife to call a guy named Frankie downtown. He and his partner owed me $1800. His partner had been killed, but he was still responsible for the debt. His reply over the phone to my wife was, "That motherfucker ain't getting a dime from me. He's going to rot in jail." I was furious when I heard his answer. That punk was scared to death of me, but because I am in here he's getting brave. He also told my wife I had killed his partner.

My wife had known I was sticking up gangsters, but as for killing people and such this too much for her. I swore to her I hadn't hurt nobody, but with me being accused of so much shit now she didn't know what to believe. She was feeling terrible about the baby and so was I. I told her when I got out we would move somewhere and I would go straight. I meant it too. I was fed up with everything. I had thought I had the answer by not sticking up legitimate people, but I saw now that the thieves and rackets guys were even bigger stool pigeons than legit people.

I did receive one bright moment while in the jail. I got a letter from some people in Connecticut saying they didn't believe the things they read about me in the papers and they were praying for me, and would never forget what I did for them. What had happened was one night I was driving to pick up my wife from the beauty parlor. On the expressway, I see this young couple with a baby, hitchhiking. I stopped to pick them up. They had had just enough money for the bus to New York and were on their way to Hartford, their home. I knew they would have a hard time hitchhiking and I tried to think of what to do. Giving them money for a bus wouldn't help because the bus stop was a long way off. I just couldn't drop them off along the expressway in hopes of their getting another ride, so I decided that my wife could always get a cab home; I'd drive them up to Hartford. They were really amazed and grateful that someone could be so nice to go out of their way like that.

I felt good being able to help them. That was the trouble with this world. Too many cold selfish bastards. We had a nice talk on the way and kind of got to know each other. It was a very good moment in my life. I read the letter many times and it made me feel I was a human being again.

Finally after 13 months of being detained in prison for a crime I hadn't committed I was released from the court. Since there were no witnesses to say I had robbed the place, they had to release me.

15

God, it was good to be out. I repeated my promise to my wife. As soon as we saved some money, we'd leave New York. I was through fucking around. I knew that, since I decided to go straight, I would have to move. Too many people now knew where I lived, and since they wouldn't believe or know I was going straight, they would figure they better get me before I got them. I was very much afraid my wife would get hurt. And she hadn't forgotten what happened to Lorraine, and it was constantly on her mind.

I joined a group that was involved with helping other ex-cons. It had just started but it was a very meaningful group. They had named themselves the Fortune Society. I was one of the very first. I was going on speaking engagements in schools and churches, everywhere we were asked. I rapped with a lot of guys just out of jail and tried to help them see jail is a nowhere experience, and we tried to help them get decent jobs.

I was very happy doing this kind of work. I have always

174

enjoyed being able to help others and more important, it gave my life some meaning. I knew though, I couldn't remain doing this. I was taking too big a risk. My name was too well known among the thieves and rackets guys. Plus I had to get out of my apartment. We were receiving threatening phone calls and my wife was in bad shape. Things were getting desperate. She was constantly afraid. I knew I had to do something.

I remembered the $1800 Frankie owed me. With that money we could leave New York and go to the Coast. I kept putting off going to see Frankie. I didn't want to see any of those guys again ever. I hated them all. The reality of my wife getting hurt if not killed was too much though. I was going to collect my money and split New York. I didn't want any trouble between Frankie and me. I would just ask for my own bread and that was that. I gave these two black guys I knew $50 apiece to come with me just to see I wasn't jumped. I brought my gun just in case Frankie tried anything. But neither of the black guys brought theirs. I wouldn't let them. I didn't want trouble.

The bar was crowded when I walked in. I asked the kid behind the bar where's Frankie. He pointed to the back. I told both black guys to stay at the bar. When I walked to the back getting ready to open the door to Frankie's office, he suddenly came out with a gun in his hand. The kid must have pressed some kind of button under the bar. As soon as Frankie saw me he started shooting. He must have thought I came down to shoot him. I went for my gun in the shoulder holster. Just as my hand reached my chest I felt the bullet punch my chest. Blood spurted everywhere. I was sure I was hit bad. I got my gun out but I couldn't hold it in my hand. I grabbed it in my left hand and started firing back. I wasn't going to die without taking this bastard with me. We couldn't have been more than fifteen feet apart; I could see every flash of his gun. I was expecting to fall any minute but I wanted to hit him before I went down. He ran back into the office and slammed the door. I was sure I had hit him but I didn't see any blood.

I turned and ran out. One of the blacks had disappeared and the other was trying to start up the car. I jumped in and told him to get the hell out of there. I told him I was hit hard. I was still holding my chest where I felt the bullet punch me, I was a bloody mess. I pulled my hand away, fully expecting to see the blood pumping from my chest. Instead I jumped in pain when I moved my hand. I looked at it; it was a bloody mess with pieces of bone sticking through. I had been shot in the hand, not the chest. The bullet had gone through my hand and struck my chest; that's why I felt the punch.

The idiot driving was panicky. He didn't know where to go and he was picking the worst streets possible. He turns on the Drive and then goes against one-way traffic. The cops are behind us by now and he pulls over. Christ, what the fuck did I get myself into? The cops surround us, search us, and shove us around. The fact that I am bleeding doesn't faze them in the least. The cop pulls my hands up behind me to cuff me and the pain is excruciating. They take us to the precinct and then they take me over to the hospital where the hand is cleaned up and bandaged. The doctor says he can't do anything more; I will need an operation to remove all the pieces of bone that were smashed. The cops assure him they will bring me to a hospital tomorrow.

Next these two detectives bring me into a small room where Frankie is sitting. His shoulder is bandaged and I learn I put one bullet through his shoulder. His is a clean bullet wound though. I tell him, "What the fuck is going on?" These cops are saying I stuck your joint up." It's obvious both these detectives are on his payroll. He's letting them listen to every thing and their manner of talking tells me I am right.

176

Frankie tells me he called the cops because he figured he had killed me and in order to clean it up for himself he had to say he shot the guy that tried to rob him. "Well now you know I'm not dead so tell them I didn't make any attempt to rob you, you motherfucker. All I wanted to do was talk to you and you pulled out your gun and shot me. These bastards want to lock me up for robbery." He says he is going to straighten it out.

One cop takes me outside while the other remains behind to talk to Frankie. My hand is killing me but I'm feeling better cause I think I am going to get cut loose. The other cop comes out and says, "So you're the one that killed his partner. We've been looking for you. We can't get you for that but we sure as shit got you for robbery." My denials are futile. No matter what I say, no one's believing me. I'm booked for robbery. I try to tell them there were over 100 people in that place, and not one can say I tried to stick it up, but they don't listen. God, I can't believe this. What is my wife going to say? That poor fucking woman. I had to be born under some kind of cursed star. How much am I expected to take?

The next day they bring me to court to be arraigned. Everything is confusion as it usually is in that courtroom. The judge asks me if I was ever arrested before and I answer, "No." The D.A. says he doesn't have my yellow sheet so he agrees to only $2500 bail. At least that's a break, I figure. The cop then tries to turn me over to the correction department, in charge of running the county jail, the Tombs. The cop there sees my hand is a bloody mess, the bandage completely soaked, and he tells the cop he better take me to the hospital first. At the hospital, the doctor wants to admit me, but the cop assures him I will be taken to Bellevue Hospital where they have a prison ward.

I'm brought back to the Tombs. I see the doctor there, a mere formality. I tell the doctor my hand is all smashed, and he says you just came from a hospital and got treated. He doesn't even take the bandage off so he has no idea what my hand looks like. I start hollering at him and the cops come and drag me out. They tell me to go on sick call the next day.

The pain is really terribly bad. They take me upstairs and put me in a cell. Between the pain and my trying to figure out how to raise some bail money the night was a nightmare. The pain completely filled my body. I was close to tears with the desperateness of the whole situation, but I was determined not to cry. I was so tired of living such a rotten life. Nothing was ever going to come out right for me. I worried about my wife knowing how she would really fall apart behind this. My hand was bleeding and though the bandage was very thick, it was now soaked with blood.

Morning came finally, and I put my name on sick call. When I got up to see the doctor he gave me some pills, saying it would stop the bleeding, and if they wanted me at the hospital they would call me. I couldn't believe such stupidity. What kind of pills stop bleeding and worse, how the fuck is Bellevue going to call for me if they don't even know about this wound? He had assumed I guess, that I had been to Bellevue already. When I explained I hadn't been there yet, and that the bones in my hand were smashed, and I needed treatment, he calmly says well, I will write to them and make an appointment for you. I was stunned at his ignorance and callousness.

They bring me back down to my cell, and fortunately, very fortunately, the cop assigned to that floor that day was a decent guy. When I told him what the doctor had said, and about giving me pills to stop the bleeding, he called the captain. When the captain came up, I had taken the bandage off my hand so he could obviously see the condition of my hand. By now it was swollen, with ugly flesh hanging and pieces of bone sticking all through the flesh. He arranged for my transfer to Bellevue Hospital.

I was immediately admitted, but it seems things still weren't to go right for me. That evening, I had gotten up from my chair to go the bathroom. When I returned my chair had been taken by some black guy. I politely asked for it back and he told me "Go fuck yourself." Man, I didn't want to fight. I couldn't fight. Once more I asked for it nicely, and got the same reply. I was fed up, everything that had happened to me in the last few days came over me. Fuck everything I said, and hit him as hard as I could with my left hand. He grabbed me and started grappling with me. I could only use one hand so I couldn't hit him again. A few minutes later the cops came over and broke it up.

These cops all knew me from the psycho side of the hospital when I caused a lot of trouble. None of them liked me. It seems I had started a fight with the nurses' pet, and the cops' flunky. He used to do their errands and serve food to them. While the cops were deciding what to do, I went over and asked for my medication because my hand was killing me. The nurse told me to wait till she was ready to give it to me. My anger and frustration caused me to blow my top. I screamed at her, "Take that medication and shove it up your cunt." Well, you just don't do things like that in jail or prison ward. She immediately told the cops she would refuse to work on the ward if I remained. Either I went or she would leave. Of course it was decided I would have to go.

They told me they were transferring me to Rikers Island Infirmary. I told them they would have to drag me off the ward, which is exactly what they did. They threw me into the back of a police van and drove me to Rikers Island. They discharged me from Bellevue without even a doctor's okay.

179

Of course they couldn't have gotten one, not once the doctor had seen my hand.

At Rikers which is also a part of the correction department (and of course they work together), I was dumped on a stretcher while they got the doctor there to sign my admittance sheet. He took one look at my hand and stated he was not going to sign any papers accepting the responsibility of my hand, it was in that bad a condition. He insisted to the guards, Rikers was only an infirmary, not a hospital, and I couldn't possibly receive proper treatment. So they had to drive me back to Bellevue. There the officers refused to accept me, and once more I was driven to Rikers. By now another doctor had come on duty, and they assured him I would only be kept at Rikers temporarily. They literally conned him into signing the papers.

The next three weeks were like a nightmare no one would dream possible. The doctor would sign the order that I was to be taken to Bellevue for treatment. This meant I had to rise and dress each morning at 5:30 A.M., sit around and wait for the van, which was a closed solid steel van with steel seats. It was designed to carry 20 people, but always there were at least 30 people or more jammed in, and those that had to stand couldn't stand upright for lack of space. Invariably there were sick junkies who would throw up, winos who would urinate and some who hadn't bathed in weeks.

Riding in that van is one of the methods a D.A. would use to coerce a man to plead guilty. The D.A. would have the man brought to court each day; he would sit in a crowded bullpen all day, the D.A. would put his name on the next day's calendar, and in the late evening the man would return, via the van back to jail. His lunch in the bullpen would be a cup of bitter tea and either a bologna or jelly sandwich. The man would have missed his visit and his chance to go to the commissary. This is a torture that wears many a man

180

down, and ultimately, he'll plead guilty to a higher charge than he ordinarily would have had to.

I had to travel to Bellevue each and every day in this van. I was in constant pain and every bounce of the van would send a jolt of severe pain through my body. It would take at least two and sometimes three hours of riding in the van before we got to Bellevue, because the van would stop at all the borough courts first. We would get to Bellevue about noon, and by that time it would be too late to see the doctor. Then I'd sit in the bullpen in Bellevue till 7 in the evening, get picked up in the van, travel to all the courts to pick up more prisoners and return to Rikers at about 11 at night. By the time we were searched and processed it would be after midnight before I got to bed. Then up at 5:30 and repeat the whole day again.

I survived this ordeal on sheer ego alone. I had no thought of the future. I concentrated on one day at a time. I was still trying to get the bail money up, which was almost an impossible task. Every time I got my hopes up that I'd get bailed out, something happened and it would fall through. It's amazing just how much the human mind can put up with.

The doctors at Rikers would do nothing more for me than give me antibiotics, and an occasional pain killer. They didn't have the facilities to do anything more and besides, they were too afraid to. In truth, they didn't want me there; they didn't want the responsibility. They would keep writing letters to Bellevue to admit me. The problem was that the interns assigned to the prison ward would listen to the cops, and the cops would tell the intern not to admit me. I was a troublemaker and a security risk. The nurse would still insist that if I was admitted she would walk off the ward.

The incredible fact is that there was a good chance I would lose my hand, and they didn't give a fuck. You the reader may find that hard to believe, but that is how callous

181

the system is. There were many inmates that lost their lives because of the same callousness and neglect. I didn't help matters much either. Perhaps if I buttered them up and kissed their ass and was apologetic I might have changed the situation. But I refused to do so. I was determined never to cop out to these bastards. Understand, if someone talked decent to me. I replied in same, but on the other hand, to those that were nasty to me, I was even nastier. I just didn't give a fuck. I had nothing to keep me going but pride.

The situation was getting worse. My hand was completely swollen out of proportion. The swelling was up to my elbow and I was getting a very bad infection. I had refused to take any more antibiotics. I told the doctors that if I couldn't get proper treatment, I didn't want any treatment. They put me on punishment for refusing medical treatment, but I knew I was pushing things to a head this way. They were fully aware that without antibiotics I would get blood poisoning, and more than likely, if I remained stubborn and refused medication I would have to have my hand amputated. And since I was in the custody of the Rikers Island Infirmary, they would be the ones responsible.

I was taking a hell of a chance and I knew it. But I had reached the point of complete desperation. Things seemed hopeless as they stood and as I have always done so many times in my life, I'd do something even crazier just to change the situation for better or worse. I was also at the point where I was thinking if I did lose my hand, I'd be able to make a deal whereby they would have to release me in order to avoid a lot of trouble with the courts and publicity and a lawsuit. My freedom meant more to me at this point than my hand.

One day I was told I was going to Bellevue and I refused to go. I was sick of that trip for nothing. I was just too beat to put up with it any longer. I was feverish and completely exhausted. The guard told me I better get my ass out of that cell and I told him go fuck himself. I was beyond the point of caring what he would do for cursing him out. A nurse came and told me I wasn't going by van, they were taking me in an ambulance, that a doctor at Bellevue had asked, or rather ordered me transferred to Bellevue. I wasn't sure whether to believe her or not, but I figured I would at least see if the ambulance part were true. I did go by ambulance, and upon reaching Bellevue, instead of sitting in the bullpen I was escorted by two gun-toting guards to another part of the hospital. This I found ridiculous, because every other inmate is escorted by one guard. After all they handcuff us anyway.

I was brought into a room where there were a lot of doctors. One of them was a hand specialist and it was he who had ordered my transfer. I found out someone had written him an anonymous letter telling him about my being denied proper medical attention. He took one look at my hand and he got very angry. He asked me who was responsible for the neglect, and all I could tell him was "the whole fucking system." He was the first person in so long that talked decently to me and his concern was genuine. I was finally being treated as a human being again. I finally let myself relax. I had been so tensed up and defensive for so long. I felt a swelling up inside and I fought back the tears. He ordered my admittance to the prison ward, and at first they told him there were no beds available. He became furious and said he would be down there in five minutes and there better be a bed available.

I was admitted and operated on. They had to take a bone graft from my hip and place it in my hand. For a while it was touch and go whether they could stem the infection in time to operate on me.

Looking back on that experience I am amazed that I feel no shock at so many people's callousness. I had experienced and seen so much brutality in my life that it was almost just what I had come to expect from society. What really fucked my head up was the fact that I had been trying to go straight, I, who was so much of an animal by society's standpoint, yet spent so much time helping people just prior to this arrest. I was capable of more compassion and humaneness than the very people who condemned me.

When my hand healed somewhat, and the pins removed, I was quickly transferred back to Rikers. My hand was still heavily bandaged and I couldn't move several fingers. I was put in the hospital ward on the sixth floor. It seemed as though I wasn't going to get bailed out. I knew I didn't have a chance in court so I began thinking of escaping. One of the windows used for fire emergency was held closed by two big padlocks. I talked about this with two other fellows I got to know who were also facing long prison terms. It was decided we would try it.

Rikers Island is off the shore of the Lower Bronx. There is another island between Rikers and the Bronx called North Brother. I was very familiar with the neighborhood. As a youth I used to swim in those waters every day. Many times I had swum out to North Brother, when they had the addicts housed there. The waters were said to be very treacherous, but I was determined to chance it, even though I was handicapped with a bad hand. At low tide, we could practically walk to North Brother, and from there I would find a piece of wood and float to the Bronx. It was a hell of a risk but at least it was a better chance than I had in court.

We decided the best plan was to steal three white uniforms from the kitchen on the floor. We would wrap these in a plastic garbage liner. When we got to the Bronx, at least we would have some clothes; we would steal a car from one of the factory parking lots and be on our way. The bakery I once worked in was right in that neighborhood, so I knew the area well.

I felt immensely better. I was doing something to survive once more. I was no longer laying around like a cow waiting for the slaughter. The excitement lifted my spirits and I felt like a man again. I was going to make it. I would wrap my hand in plastic so as not to get it wet. We decided it was each man for himself once we got into the water. If one couldn't make it that was his tough luck. We knew the penalties of getting caught. We would get our asses kicked, solitary confinement, and a longer prison term. So once we got into the water there was no turning back. It was either make it or drown.

Climbing down the sheet-made rope wouldn't be bad. There was an overhanging ledge halfway down. I knew I could make it with one hand. The difficult part of the break was that we had to do everything in one night. There was no way we could break the lock without the others on the ward knowing what was happening. We figured no one would want to risk ratting right out in the open, for fear of reprisals from the others. The guard never came on the ward at night, and we didn't think anyone would have the balls to go up to the locked door and start hollering for the guard. If we left right after the midnight change of shift, we wouldn't be discovered missing until breakfast at 5:30 A.M.

Each day I read the newspapers so as to find out when it would be low tide. Finally the time came. Everything was ready. We had to break the locks early in the evening while the TV was on so the guard wouldn't hear it. Since I couldn't break the locks with my one hand I would be the one who would turn up the TV just at the moment of stress on the lock. We had a steel bar that was smuggled up to us from a reliable person. Once the locks were broken, we'd just play cool till midnight. As soon as I saw him ready to pop the lock I reached over and turned the volume high. Crack went the lock.

Immediately everybody turned and saw what was happening. Before I could tell the guys to mind their own business or they would get their heads broke, one of the onlookers said, "Listen, fellows, why don't we all just forget it and give the cats a chance to make it." Man, that was beautiful of him. Then with a hint of threat in his voice, he concluded, "I mean, I'm sure we ain't got no rats in here." Crack went the other lock. We were set. Nothing to do now but wait.

My nerves were tingling with the excitement. In a few days I would be long gone from New York. I knew a racket boss I could kidnap easily and get 50 grand for. And if any of his punks got in my way I'd blow them away. I had absolutely nothing to lose.

We watched TV till 11 o'clock when they shut it off. The inmate nurse came around to give out medication. The guard stood, as usual, at the door. No one made an attempt to talk to him. That was good. We were safe. The nurse left the ward, the door was locked and the lights went out.

For a moment I thought of the dark, cold river and what drowning would be like. I quickly pushed it from my mind and replaced it with the image of me, with a gun in my hand, telling the motherfucker he better get someone to come up with 50 grand or he would be a dead bastard.

Suddenly, the lights in the ward came on. Immediately, the ward was filled with guards. One of them went directly to the window where the locks had been broken. They knew about it, the bastards. How? They ordered us all out of bed and to stand at the foot of the beds while they tore up the place searching. We had everything hidden in the garbage can in the bathroom. In no time at all they found the stuff. Shit, what a motherfucking drag. Just once I'm going to plan something that works.

They called us out one at a time and grilled us. It seems

186

they didn't know who was involved. The captain said he would bet his life I was involved in it, but I showed him my hand and said how would I ever be able to climb down a rope, much less swim with my hand in such useless condition. The grilling went on all night. The windup was I was the only person locked in a cell. Nothing else. I wasn't beaten or severely threatened. Just put in a cell. I really bluffed him out with my hand. I guess he figured no one would be crazy enough to try that stunt with a hand as fucked up as mine was.

But still, because I was considered a ringleader on the ward, and a security risk, the next morning I was told I was being transferred to the Tombs. Before I left in the morning, I found out how the guards learned of the escape plan. The guy whose bed was directly in front of the window got scared he would be hassled by the guards and they would blame him because it was by his window, so he had told the nurse to tell the guard someone was trying to escape. Later, when the guards questioned him, he swore he didn't know who broke the locks nor how long they had been broken. He just happened to be looking out the window and discovered it. At least the fuck didn't name any names.

I was in the Tombs about two weeks when one day my name was called out. I was told to pack up, I had been bailed out. I couldn't believe it. I wondered who could have bailed me out. I gave my belongings away to those that needed it and went downstairs to be processed. I was scared that something would go wrong; what I couldn't imagine, but I just couldn't believe my luck. Each minute I had to wait seemed like an eternity. I just know some thing is going to go wrong, I kept thinking. For God's sake, hurry it up, I said to the guard, under my breath, of course.

Finally, they led me through the locked gates that separated the inside from the outside. Then I saw who had bailed me out. David, the guy who started Fortune Society. I never understood why he took the risk of bailing me out. After all, I had enough reasons to jump bail. I was facing a long prison term, yet he had enough faith in me to bail me out.

This was a very strange period in my life. I knew was going to prison eventually, even though for a crime I hadn't committed. I had all the reason in the world to jump bail, but I just couldn't. David was the first person in my life to put himself on the line for me, and I just couldn't screw him. Many times I thought of ripping someone off, and giving David the bail money he put up; I didn't because he was too good for me to fuck up. Besides, it would certainly have looked bad for Fortune if the first person they bailed out jumped.

So I worked in his office, answering letters and counseling guys that just came out of prison. I also did many speaking engagements. Then I got a job working for a guy that saw me on a TV show. He hired me as sort of office manager and trusted me completely. He was a fantastic person, the kind you wouldn't believe existed. There was no way in hell I could screw him. He and David are both responsible for my not returning to crime. It was while working on this job that months later I got taken for a ride by my "friend."

PART TWO

16

My thoughts of the past were interrupted by the sounds of the cops coming into my room. Quickly I closed my eyes and pretended to be asleep. I heard the nurse say come back in an hour. I lay there thinking life wasn't worth the hassle. I knew what was in store for me, what with the questioning and the threats, and above all, I knew they could do just about anything they wanted with me. I had no bread for a decent lawyer, and I could easily see me spending the next 15 or 20 years in prison.

I thought back to the night the shooting happened. I had met my friend Jerry the night before. He had recently been released from prison. We had been very close for eight years there, and a friendship in prison has much more import than a friendship on the streets.

We had met in a mutual friend's bar. We had some drinks and I told him what I was doing. I had been working as an office manager, and doing volunteer work helping other ex-cons try to get a new start. He then asked to speak to me in private (Lori was with me), and we excused our-

191

selves. He asked me what I was doing for bread, and I told him I wasn't fucking around anymore. I had tried to take some small-town rackets guy off, and as usual it was a big disappointment, so I made up my mind to quit. I would never take off any legit guy again, and I was tired of the whole hassle.

Then he hit me with a proposition. He knew this racket guy, an acquaintance of his whom he had to meet the next night, and the guy had a sure 100 grand in his house. He wanted me to help him take the guy off. I guess Jerry knew all the time I wouldn't refuse to help him. He had done a lot of favors for me in prison and he was the closest friend I had. I did tell him though, that from past experiences I doubted if the guy had all that money in the house. He assured me he knew for a fact, and I believed him because I wanted to believe him. Plus I was glad that I was able to help him. So we agreed to meet the next night. I asked Jerry about his cousin Lenny who was becoming a big narcotics pusher. He said his cousin wasn't doing anything for him, just telling him to wait and stringing him along. Lenny didn't like me but he wouldn't dare show his dislike. I had fucked up his Mafia image several times.

I took Lori home and she told me she didn't like my friends. I couldn't ride the middle of the fence, she said, and if I was going straight I couldn't keep going back to see my old crowd. How right she was. But I was torn. I really dug the new legit friends I had made; they were more for real. I enjoyed the work I was doing. I was helping people. I was doing something good, and getting a great deal of satisfaction from it. I was needed and important to some people, and I loved Lori. I would have cut off my arm for her and given her everything I had, but I just couldn't resist going back to see my old friends. After all, I had spent many years in prison with these guys, and we had shared grotesque experiences.

192

It was something I could never share with legit people. Without these old friends, I had no past life. And I liked the excitement, the fast life.

Lori couldn't understand it, but even so, she never hassled me or carped at it. We made beautiful love that night. Lori was one of the most desirable women anyone could hope to meet. One of the very few totally good women, and extremely beautiful to boot.

I left her the next evening, promising I would return in two hours at most. I went over to my house to pick up some stuff and also to tell Connie I wouldn't be home that night. Connie was a beautiful girl, totally in love with me. I dug her also; she gave me a lot I needed. She was half my age, and she gave me the youth I missed. She wasn't happy with me being out so much. I hated making her unhappy, and causing her to cry. How can I explain the hurt inside me when I made her unhappy, and yet something compelled to do other things. She was crying when I left that evening, and I wished to God as I closed the door, that I could go back in and hold her and be totally content inside with myself. But this compulsion that was an integral part of my life was too strong inside me.

As I got in my car and started driving to meet Jerry, the old feeling of excitement arose within me. It completely blocked out any guilt feelings I had. I got to the bar about an hour early, and while waiting I started rapping with three good-looking chicks. They were going to a party and wanted me to go with them. I told them I was waiting for a friend and perhaps in a couple hours we would meet them at the party. Jerry came in and sat with me and the girls. It was obvious two of the girls really dug me and made it plain I'd have an exciting night if I met them later in the evening. We got up to leave promising to meet them later.

We were leaving my car at the bar so I followed Jerry to

his. When I saw this guy Bill sitting in the car, Jerry told me he was going with us. I didn't ask any questions, but I wondered why the hell we needed another guy. I was sure Jerry and I could do this alone, and now we would have to cut another guy in on a share of the bread. For a moment a strange feeling came over me. I couldn't put my finger on it, and since I trusted Jerry more than any other guy I knew I pushed the feeling out of my mind and sat back to relax.

The plan was for Jerry to knock on the door and since the cat knew Jerry he would open the door to let him in. Then we would all go in. The fact that we would probably have to kill this guy didn't especially bother me. I knew of him and he had often had quite a few people killed himself. We drove to the town and Jerry got lost in the dark, or did he? I thought so then, but now I can see what he was trying to do. Anyway, we pulled up in front of the house, and me and Bill got out on the passenger side.

It was very dark and we started walking towards the front of the house. Jerry was a few steps behind us and I thought he was catching up. Suddenly I felt as if a lightening bolt had hit me. My head was filled with lights, and I felt something hit me in the head. I turned and saw the flame from a gun and felt a hot poker go into my side. Immediately I realized this was a knockoff. My face must have shown the disbelief that Jerry would be the one to kill me; I remember saying, "Not you, Jerry." My instinct made me grab Bill to swing him in front of me as a shield. Then I realized he was pulling a gun from his belt. I started fighting with him trying to grab the gun which was still in the holster. As I was grappling with him, I heard more explosions and felt the bullets hitting me. At the moment I felt no pain. I was like a maniac. I snatched the gun from Bill. Fortunately for him it was still encased in a holster, and I couldn't get at the trigger. He hollered to Jerry, "Look out, he's got my gun," and the two of them ran like hell to the car.

It was at that moment I fell. I believe my anger and frustration kept me from passing out. I didn't want to die unavenged. I wanted them to go with me. My only thoughts were not to let them get away. The car lights came on and the beams lit me up in the darkness. The car was rushing at me. With an effort that can only be described as herculean I willed my body to roll out of the way at the last moment. The car roared by me, barely inches from my face. I tried getting the gun from the holster, but one arm was completely paralyzed. The pain was excruciating. I used my teeth to open the snap, got out the gun, aimed it at the rapidly disappearing car and fired till the gun was empty.

Then I realized it was all over and I relaxed surprisingly easy. As I lay there, the upper part of my body filled with pain. Then a fantastic feeling of euphoria began enveloping my body beginning at my feet. I could feel it coming up my body beginning at my feet. I could feel it coming up my body and slowly the pain disappeared. I was experiencing the greatest high of my life. I knew I was going to die, and felt a sense of relief, glad that the hassle of life was going to end. Sirens brought me back to reality, and I tried to tell them to just leave me alone. I heard people yelling, "He's shot, he's shot," and felt people pulling at my body to get me on a stretcher. The hassle was getting to me. Can't a man even die in peace?

I woke up in a hospital emergency room. It seemed as if a hundred faces surrounded me. A glaring light above my eyes blinded me and I moved my head to escape it. Instantly the pain hit me. Cops were yelling in my ear, "Who did it? Don't let them get away with it. Tell us now before it is too late." Someone else was asking me if I was Catholic and

195

wanted a priest, and then a priest was bending over me making the sign of the cross. I told him I was Jewish, and he said "Never mind son, say your confession and make your peace with God." I thought back to the times when I had told myself, if a priest comes when I am dying, I'll tell him to go fuck himself. But I didn't feel anger now. I replied very calmly that God didn't help me when I was alive and needed him, so I'm certainly not going to ask his help now.

I lay there, totally oblivious to the cops, the nurses, to everything. I was willing myself to die, feeling pleased that I wasn't scared and was dying like a man. A doctor felt my pulse and I could see him shake his head, relaying the message to the others in the room: I didn't have a chance. I heard a cop's voice asking me if I wanted anyone to be with me—family, friend or anyone. At first I said no, just leave me alone. Then I realized I didn't want to die alone. I didn't want to leave life a nonbeing, a nobody, as I lived it. Alone and unloved in death. The meaning of the words came to me and a terrible feeling of despair came over me. I gave them Lori's phone number. Shortly a cop came to my side and told me they were sending a car to pick her up and bring her here. At that moment I fought to live. I didn't want her to see a dead body. And I wanted to die in the presence of her love and warmth.

They transferred me to another hospital equipped with brain surgery equipment. The neurosurgeon at the hospital happened to be one of the best. He also was a very humane person and took quite a liking to me. He said my body was in absolutely perfect condition and I was healing amazingly well. One bullet was left in my back to be removed later.

I enjoyed being in the hospital. It was quite a relief just being able to lie there and rest. But that wasn't to last long. I received a letter from the court in Manhattan. They had revoked my bail because I hadn't shown up in court. This had to be a mistake; I wasn't scheduled to be in court for another month. I called my bondsman. He said it was true. The D.A., learning I was in the hospital and incapable of moving, had moved my case up. I called the precinct where the warrant had been sent and explained my situation, but they said I had better be in court Thursday. Christ, how the hell was I going to make it? My only chance at beating the case in Manhattan was to remain on bail for a while.

I explained the situation to the doctor. He called the D.A.'s office and said I wasn't in condition to be released from the hospital. The D.A. ignored him completely. There wasn't much more the doctor could do but he did write a letter to the judge, giving me a copy. Against his wishes I signed myself out of the hospital the day before my scheduled court appearance. I was in very bad shape physically. True, the wounds were healing rapidly, but damage caused by the bullet in the head would take some time to heal. I couldn't see well, the left side of my body was partially paralyzed, thereby preventing me from walking with any stability, and I stammered quite a bit.

Before leaving the hospital, the cops assigned to investigate the shooting told me that unless I cooperated with them they were charging me with possession of a pistol, the one found in my hand when I lay in the street. They also said that they could make quite a case against me, and I didn't stand a chance in court. With my record, I knew I had a good chance of going to prison for 15 to 20 years. I just couldn't believe this was happening to me. Couldn't they believe I was the victim? During the ride back to the city, my head was filled with so much shit, I was totally confused. I thought of just jumping bail, going on the lam and going back to kidnapping mob guys. But if I jumped bail, my friend who had enough faith in me to have bailed me out with his last dollars, would lose the money. I didn't want to hang him up.

197

He was a square cat who somehow knew or sensed the real me deep inside.

I decided what I needed was a good lawyer, and while I didn't have the bread for one I thought I knew how to get it. As soon as I hit the city I called the people who put Jerry up to shooting me. I told them unless they came up with five grand for a lawyer, I was going to cooperate with the police and testify against Jerry. There was no way in hell I could convince anybody I was trying to go straight and yet still refuse to cooperate. They would naturally continue to believe I was still involved with crime. I told them point blank, if one of us had to go to jail for 20 years, it was going to be Jerry, not me. So it was up to them to get the bread to me. They were lucky all I was asking for was five grand. I also ran down how because of this bullshit, my bail had been revoked, and since they had the connections they could see to it my bail was reinstated.

I then went over to Lori's. She changed the bandages and even in my weakened condition we made love that night as if it would be the last time ever. It was impossible for me to sleep that night, what with my body hurting in so many places, and my mind busy with wondering what was going to happen in court in the morning. My first inclination was not to show up. Rather, I would go find Jerry's cousin and take him off, get the bread, use it for a lawyer and show up in court the next day. That would have been the best thing to do, except for one thing. I knew damn well I wouldn't find him. Until he knew for sure that I was in jail, he wouldn't be anywhere in the city. So I figured I'd take my chances in court. Once the judge saw the condition I was in, and once he read the doctor's letter that I should be in a hospital, I felt he would reinstate my bail. After all, I didn't do anything wrong. What a fool I was!

I got out of the cab and looked up at the monstrous

building that represented Justice. Disgust filled me completely. I thought of my past life, and thought of all the other people I knew that got fucked throughout their lives. If I had a bomb large enough, I would have blown the whole fucking thing up. Walking up the steps I felt dizzy and suddenly my body crashed sideways. My equilibrium was still way off and I had been getting dizzy pretty often, but usually there was something to hold on to till it passed. This time there was nothing so I just fell. What was I doing here, I thought. Nobody in their right mind would be out in the condition I was in.

I got up to the courtroom and saw the Legal Aid I knew. He told me the District Attorney had a hard on for me and moved the case before this judge whom he knew. That's the story of "justice" in a nutshell. The D.A. tries to get the case in front of one of his judges, and the lawyer tries to get the case in front of one that he knows or one that is lenient. Your sentence is going to be determined by which does the most manipulating. Since I didn't have my own lawyer, and since the Legal Aid lawyers have their problems—heavy work load, insufficient experience, or just not caring—few people represented by Legal Aid ever get a fair play in court.

I was called up before the judge, and immediately the D.A. launched a long tirade. I was a mobster, I was involved in a shootout upstate, I was involved with gambling and narcotics. This was absolute bullshit. Out and out lies. I started to speak, but all I could do was stammer. The judge cut me off and said, "Bail revoked. Take him away." I continued trying to speak, but the judge wouldn't listen to anything. Get him out of here, he ordered. I couldn't believe this was happening. I looked at the Legal Aid lawyer, but the judge wouldn't let him speak either.

I was brought to the Tombs, stripped down in the bullpen and assigned a cell upstairs. Before going upstairs we

199

all had to see the doctor. Every inmate in the place considered this formality a joke. You saw the doctor for about five seconds and were ushered out. Even the guards considered this a waste of time. I tried to tell the doctor I had been shot five times just weeks ago, and was supposed to be in a hospital. He told me to report to sick call the next day. I had been assigned an upper bunk. I couldn't even climb up to it. Fortunately my cell mate switched bunks with me. I had no sheets, nor blankets. One usually had to be there a week before you got sheets. It was winter and freezing. I lay there shivering all night.

The next day after futile efforts to get medical attention, I refused to lock in my cell. I demanded to see a Captain. This really nasty cop told me he would break my head if I didn't get in the cell. At this point I just didn't care what happened. My situation was already bad enough; it couldn't get worse. I told the guard if he put a hand on me I would do my best to tear out his eye. He would have to kill me. Fortunately the other guard was a bit more understanding. When I told him about my head wound and other injuries, he said he would call the Captain. The Captain came up and said there was nothing he could do. I would have to see the doctor in the morning. He said he would make out a report and the doctor would be sure to get it. If another Captain had told me this I would doubt very much anything being done, but this Captain I knew. There was nothing else to do but go along with it. I didn't get to the hospital until three weeks later, and then only because I had a seizure.

At Bellevue, I got my first bit of luck in ages. The admitting intern on the prison ward, upon hearing my story of being shot, asked me the doctor's name that operated on me. When he told me he knew the doctor and was studying under him I knew then I would get some treatment. The next day the intern came to my bed and told me he had

200

talked with my doctor. He assured me he would keep me in the hospital as long as possible. Bellevue prison ward has a reputation of discharging prisoner patients much too soon. They do this so they can get another prisoner into the ward to practice on. Many, many prisoners were operated on unnecessarily, just so the interns could get some experience.

I learned that many legitimate people were showing up in court for me trying to get my bail reinstated, but with no success. Having had no previous dealings with the court system, their impression of our judicial system was that there was fair play and justice. After having seen and heard what was going on with my case—the D.A. outright lying and the judge refusing to listen to anyone on my behalf—they expressed outright shock that these things were happening. I told them such things happen hundreds of times.

My case was moved for trail before one of the worst judges. I still hadn't heard anything but promises from Jerry's cousin. I again promised I would testify against Jerry at his trial and state he was the one that shot me, that they better hurry and help me. The problem was that they felt if they helped me get out, I would come after them. And they damn sure knew I would get them.

I tried every stall possible so I wouldn't have to stay before this judge. He had told me if I got convicted he would give me the maximum 25 years. The only plea he would offer was 15 years. I damn sure wasn't going to take that. The Legal Aid lawyer made a plea that I be sent for psychiatric examination since the tests showed brain damage as a result of the bullet. The judge denied him. The lawyer stated that in that case he would ask to withdraw because in his mind I was in no condition to stand trial. The judge then assigned another lawyer to me. Two weeks later he came to me and said he was going to ask to withdraw. He told me right out the D.A. was determined to get me. And since he wasn't getting paid, it wouldn't be worth his while making enemies with the court by exposing the dirt the D.A. was pulling to get me a stiff sentence.

Everyone connected with the case, the three lawyers I had at different times, the cops on the case, and the cops handling the case upstate, all said the same thing in so many words. Somebody was paying this D.A. off to get me hung. I very much believed it. Too many people didn't want me out on the streets. I had a crazy reputation and they knew it wouldn't be easy for them to get me first. Jerry's cousin was in a bind also. He was afraid to help me get out. At the same time, even if he wanted to sacrifice Jerry, other good friends of Jerry's were putting pressure on asking why was Jerry still in jail. And that if all it took to get Jerry out was to help me, it better be done.

Finally came the day of Jerry's trial. I was brought up-state the day before, and the D.A. asked me if I was going to testify against Jerry. I asked him what was in it for me. Could he make a deal down in Manhattan for me? He said he wouldn't promise anything but he would do the best he could. He said he had tried to talk to the D.A. but the guy seemed obsessed with getting me.

Next day I was called to the stand. In truth I didn't know what I was going to do on the witness stand. I wasn't really angry at Jerry. His cousin had told him a lot of shit about me shooting someone close to Jerry and Jerry had believed it. I couldn't forget how close Jerry was to me in prison and all he had done for me. From the witness stand I looked down at him. He was flanked by two sharp lawyers. I wanted to tell him the best lawyers in the world couldn't help him now. The only person able to help him stay out of prison for the next fifteen years was me. Me, the same guy you tried to kill!

After some preliminary questions the D.A. asked me if I saw the person or persons that shot me on such and such

202

night. Even at this point I still didn't know what I was going to say. Sending Jerry to prison wasn't going to give me any satisfaction. After knowing what prison was like I wouldn't be able to send anyone there. And testifying against him just because his cousin was fucking me around wouldn't be fair. I thought of all this while I looked at the jury, and then I looked at Jerry. He seemed to be holding his breath. Certainly his sister and mother in the back were holding their breaths.

The D.A. again asked me the question. I almost laughed at how dramatic the whole scene was. Everybody waiting for me. To hear what I had to say. A rare moment in my life when people were going to pay attention to what I had to say. I relished the moment. I turned to the judge and stated I felt sick and would like to see a doctor. I knew I could call the shots to some extent. He replied, "Just answer the question," but I refused and insisted I see a doctor. His face turned red. The D.A. hollered I was playing games with the courtroom. He was right. Fuck this courtroom and fuck this system. Justice was a mockery.

The judge was forced to call a recess and order the attendants to take me to a doctor who gave me some pills for seizures and aspirin. I was quickly brought back to the courthouse. Before I went into the courtroom the cops started pressuring me. Why should I care about this bastard? He tried to kill me. He didn't care a damn about me. And think of the others he'll kill. An animal like him belongs in prison. I pictured these same cops saying the same things about me, as so many other cops and judges had.

The court convened and I was led to the witness stand. I was reminded I was still under oath. "Do you see the person or persons that shot you on such and such night?" Again I let the suspense mount and then I answered. "I do not remember getting shot," I replied, staring right into Jerry's eyes. I

203

saw him release the breath he was holding and a small grin appear on his face. The D.A. was furious. Don't I remember being in the hospital? Where did I think all those bullet wounds came from? I replied I don't remember getting shot. He asked for a recess and got it.

When I was brought outside the courtroom he threatened to bring perjury charges against me. He also swore he would get me for having a gun. At that point I just didn't care. I told him, "Fuck you, do what you want." After about a half hour wait, I learned the case against Jerry was dismissed. I was returned to my own problems in Manhattan.

I learned that my stalling tactics had worked. The judge was tied up in a lengthy trial and I was assigned a new judge. This judge happened to be one that didn't believe in long sentences and more important, he was one that understood there was always more to a case than just what appeared in the indictment sheet. After learning all the details involved and allowing character witnesses to appear in my behalf, he allowed me to plea to the lowest degree and promised a lenient sentence and possible discharge. It helped too that one of my best friends went to the same synagogue as the judge.

When I was returned for sentencing, the judge said he had in mind to release me on probation, that while my record was a terrible one, the work I was doing preceding this arrest and while on bail was such that he felt I was rehabilitated. The problem facing him though was that the probation department stated they didn't want to accept me. So the judge gave me a term of one year to four years. A few months earlier, in front of the other judge I would have been delighted to get four years, but now I didn't feel that good. After all, I was still getting four years for a crime that never happened.

I was shipped to Sing Sing a few days later, and I knew

I would have a rough time. Many of the old friends I had in prison heard a lot of stories about me and didn't know what to believe. I was supposed to have been shot because I ratted on someone. I was supposed to have ratted on Jerry. I was supposed to have hurt some good people. Any one of these was enough to cause their not talking to me. I wasn't going to be able to do this bit as one of the inside people. I was to be an outcast.

I didn't really care that much. By now I knew just how full of shit they all were. I was just hoping none of them would fuck with me, call me stool pigeon or any other insults. I knew then I would have to hurt somebody, and this I didn't want to do. I wanted to get out of prison as soon as possible. Not get a new term for seriously hurting someone. Also, friends of mine outside were trying to get me transferred to an experimental therapeutic community. It was real easy there. Unlike the atmosphere in the prisons with the strict regimentation and discipline, the experimental center had a more relaxed atmosphere. You were treated more like a human than an animal. This was important to me, because I didn't want to return to the streets a bitter, angry madman which I would have if I spent my term in the prisons.

Epilogue

I've been "out" now for more than three years. It's by far the longest period of freedom in my life. By freedom I mean not in a prison of bricks and bars. True, I'm out amid "society" now, but as we all know, there are two societies. One for those that have, and one for those that don't have. When I read of bribe taking, and graft, and theft, by our leaders, the politicians, when such crimes as the Attica murders take place, and the people accept these things, I feel my freedom is still being deprived.

When I read of the terrible child abuse committed in foster homes and the public's apathy towards it, and the atrocities still being committed in juvenile detention facilities and the public's indifference, I can never feel free, because I suffer and I hurt all over again as I read or hear of each incident. I hurt for two reasons; one is because I've "been there" and the second reason is because I know something can be done about it, if enough people care. If other people, other lives, and our feelings toward humans were first and foremost in the meaning of our lives, things would be changed. But unfortunately, money and power and position seem to be the dominant factor in our lives. But I am not here to lecture, so on with the story.

On the day of my release, there was a great snowstorm. The train ride took 13 hours. I got to the city a little after midnight and as I walked out to the streets I thought to myself, "Well, this is your last chance." It was a little scary. There was nothing about the city to reinforce a good feeling in myself. It was cold and dreary, and that's exactly how I felt about myself.

I had forty dollars in my pocket with which to find a place to live and feed myself till I got a job and my first paycheck. I felt as if it were a survival test, where they put you on this island and tell you use your wits and survive. Except on an island there are bushes and berries and plants for one to eat; in the city there are stop signs, fire hydrants and concrete—hardly digestible.

I went on exactly 31 job interviews with no success. In each job I was more than qualified, but then comes the question: "Where have you worked before," and 20 years is a long gap to fill in with phony jobs. I was broke, disgusted and hungry. Many times I said to myself, I must be crazy, thinking I can make it straight. I lay in my hotel room thinking how easy it would be to go out and rip someone off. There was no one I could talk to. I was never able to discuss my feelings with someone, nor was it part of my makeup to ask someone for help. I have always been quick to help others and glad to do so, but there is a barrier inside when it comes to asking others for help. I guess what really kept me straight at the time was the fact I was going out on many speaking engagements for Fortune Society, to schools, churches, meetings, etc. After each engagement, the parents and kids would come up to me and thank me, and the warmth with which I was received was very gratifying. I knew I was doing some good and it made me feel important.

My parole officer was giving me a lot of leeway and this helped. I was in no mood to be hassled by one of them. He had told me I was beyond the stage where lecturing me would do any good, so he just let me come in, say hello, accepted anything I said and then I would leave. I had gotten my driver's license without telling him about it, and because I had the license I finally got a job driving a truck.

The pay was good, though the work was frustrating. I couldn't deal with the aggravation of midtown traffic, through which I had to go to deliver stuff each day. Many times I would explode and curse other drivers out. And if they dared to curse back, on several occasions I got out of my truck and physically threatened them. Their rudeness and aggressiveness was too much for me to cope with. I hadn't let myself get this aggravated in prison, and I would take it personal if a driver cut me off. For the same reason, I still haven't learned how to ride the subways. The rudeness and callousness and the pushing and shoving gets to me. And if I turn around and call someone a motherfucker for deliberately pushing me, everyone looks at me as if I was some kind of animal. I mean it's okay if they shove you, but if you curse or threaten, you're some kind of nut.

I was finally transferred to the out-of-town deliveries. This was really nice, and now I dug the job. I broke my ass for the company, and I was saving a few bucks. Then the company went out of business. Fortunately I was able to land a job immediately, working for the city as a Drug Counselor.

This was the kind of work that appealed to me. This was what I was best suited for. And while I was able to work on my own so to speak, I was able to reach a lot of people. Kids and parents alike would want to come in to rap with me. I

208

put everything into this job. And it was great listening to everyone say how good I was. I was good for one reason only: I hadn't forgotten what I went through. I never forgot where I came from, and I knew what it was not to have someone to talk with.

Then I got promoted and because of the volume of people I was reaching, my department was expanded. And I quickly saw what it was like to work in a bureaucracy. I quickly became aware of the petty jealousies, the duplication of work, and the nonwork in many of the offices. Most of the bosses in the agency where I worked gave less than a fuck about helping the addict. All they were interested in was the power of their position, and the publicity.

Publicity was the key word. Trying to justify the amount of money they were spending was their main objective. If 100 people called my department for assistance of some kind, I was told to make the figure 300, so it could be published in the paper. Of course I refused to do this. I would receive many complaints regarding a particular drug program. I would make out a report, and hand it in to my superior. His attitude was "Well, there's nothing we can do about it." This infuriated me, because since our agency was funding the program we damn sure could do something about it. It was simply a question of not wanting to "rock the boat." Meantime, the only people getting hurt by this attitude were the very people we were supposed to be helping.

I began hating my job and I would go home each night with a tight gut. I felt like a hypocrite, something I had never been in my life. I had always hated the "system" and now I hated it more than ever. And worse, now I was part of the very system I hated! I was a part of the indifference of the system.

Meantime, I was given still yet another promotion. But I felt far from happy about it. I didn't want to be caught up

209

in the security of the job like everyone was telling me. Perhaps in any other type of business I could let myself fuck around on the job, but certainly not in this field. Many others on the job agreed with me, but they would tell me to be cool. "There's nothing you can do about the system." Well, I found that to be true. My reports would be shuffled around and then "lost." Figures would be manipulated and exaggerated and then published. Worse, these figures would supposedly be coming from my department.

At night, I would think of all the people in prison that wouldn't necessarily be there except for the callousness of the system. And I thought of all the people that would wind up in prison because they called for help, but found none. My anger and hatred was becoming alive again, and I knew this was dangerous for me. I had to get out but like so many of us I found myself caught up in the security of having a job, and the fear of being unemployed. But this was compromising with myself and I was never able to do that, so I took my vacation and never went back. And still yet, while on vacation, I was given a promotion. My new job would consist of me sitting in an office with practically nothing to do, and five others to do it with. I feel this was a token, because I had threatened to go to the newspapers about the big ripoff of the public's money. I had talked this idea over with some others but we all agreed that the only people that would be hurt were the little people. The bosses would always be able to cover themselves and would always be able to get good jobs in the bureaucracy. I've had the opportunity to look at the "system" from both sides now and it stinks more than I ever thought before. I want no part of it, and I am determined to escape from it as much as possible.

One question I have been asked hundreds of times is: "What made you become rehabilitated? When did you de-

210

cide to change?" People ask this question as if there was some point in my life when I sat down and said: "Well, I've been a bad boy and it's time now to be a better person and be rehabilitated. I've learned my lesson."

Let me make one thing clear! I am still the same person now as I've always been. I don't feel any different now. The only thing I regret is the years in prison. I don't regret the crimes, and I'm not sorry I did them. I only did what the system taught me. I am still very disillusioned, very disgusted, and still hate the system for its indifference and callousness. I am still angry and full of fight inside. There's just one difference now. I know I can't fight the system and win. I can't change it. If I were to kill five hundred people, it wouldn't change a damn thing. The machine would keep rolling.

And that's the sad part. You either become a part of the machine, a robot, or you get rolled over. I don't steal now, not out of fear of getting caught or because it's wrong to steal, but because the money isn't going to give me any better peace of mind. The reality that things are fucked up is still going to be in my head. Every time I go into the bank and see someone make a large withdrawal the first thing I think of is how to rip them off. I guess that will always be a part of me. When things are going bad and I feel uptight, the first thing I think of is going back to crime. It's always in the back of my head. And that's where it will stay.

I still find myself two very different people. I love the country, the quietness, and my friends in the country. They are a whole different type of people. Yet, I still enjoy the "fast" life: the gambling, the late hours, the recklessness of fast living, always on the verge of getting involved in a "shady" deal, but never quite. The excitement overcomes the depression inside me. It makes me forget my daily fight to survive. I would imagine there are many others like me, frustrated with the present conditions and situation and feeling helpless and hopeless for not being able to change them. So where do we fit in? We're just not capable of becoming one of the sheep and following along.

I thought I had the answer one time. I would be concerned with only the world I lived in and could do something about. Anything outside that world I wouldn't worry about. Never mind the people in Bangladesh, never mind Vietnam, forget about the corruptness of the leaders. I mean it's a shame but there is nothing I can do about it so why let it bother me. But that didn't do it. I couldn't ignore or block such things out. I am a human being and human beings have feelings. So of course I have to feel upset when I read or hear of something unpleasant. I wonder how other people deal with it. The caring sensitive people. I know how the insensitive deal with it.

I am all too aware that nobody said life was going to be fair. And I keep reminding myself of that. But damn it, you get tired of getting fucked around. You get tired of nothing going your way, no matter how you try, or what your intentions are. I've never been a lucky person. And I keep saying my luck is bound to change. But I don't believe it. Some are lucky, some aren't. Speaking realistically, the old saying, "you make your own luck" is a crock of shit. I'm not looking to win the sweepstakes. Or strike it big. I'm just tired of fighting tooth and nail to survive. I'd like a little wind behind me to help push me along over the rough spots, instead of running head-on into a gale.

But you can't erase 20 years of prison. Other people aren't going to forget it, and I certainly can't. The physical scars from the beatings have all disappeared, but the mental ones haven't. Perhaps they never will. Yet somehow I've got to learn not to let them affect me. But how? Perhaps the judge that told me prison would be a good thing for me, since he had the answer then, maybe he's got the answer now.

Many terrible things can be said about the prison system, all of them true, but I believe the worst thing about sending a man to prison for any number of years is that the punishment doesn't end on the day of his release. For years afterwards he will have to endure further punishment. Innumerable jobs will be denied him; credit will be difficult to obtain; he will have to wait years before applying for reinstatement of his citizenship status, which is taken away upon imprisonment; he will have to suffer the prejudice of other people who will never forget he is an ex-convict. And equally damaging to his well-being, it will take years for the mental scars to heal up inside him.

It's not the bars nor the stone walls that tear a man up. He can always rationalize that he did something wrong and the walls and bars are his punishment. But how can he rationalize away the daily degradation, the brutal and sadistic treatment he is subjected to day after day, year after year, especially by people who claim to be his betters? People that commit acts that even he is not capable of. How can you ever forget being treated worse than an animal? Is it any wonder it takes years after release, sometimes never, before we can get ourselves together? And during those interim years, we hurt and suffer every day. And too many times the conflict and struggle is too strong, and nothing was ever done to prepare us for this battle, so we take the easy way out. We go back to stealing, *not* for profit or to get away, but really with the intention of getting caught.

The majority of men I met in prison have a better basic sense of honesty than the people outside. What about the shopowner who marks his prices up outrageously and then

213

swears they're the lowest prices in town, or swears what you are buying is genuine when it's not? Or the cab driver that drives you around in circles to run the meter up, or the guy that sells you his car swearing nothing is wrong with it, and you buy it and find out it needs a major repair? Or the land-lords that take your rent and then don't give you the proper services, or the people that manufacture defective goods just so you have to pay further for repairs?

Man, this society is full of cheaters, and cheating is steal-ing—only they do it in a conniving way and then feel pleased with themselves saying what good businessmen they are. Myself and a lot of other men in prison wouldn't be able to do this. I can't steal in a sneaky way. At least I steal "up front." You know I'm stealing from you. If you cheat and steal in one way, you're not much different from the guy that steals openly. You are both thieves. Get my point? It's okay to deprive a man of his pride and hope, but let that same man slip into your garden and steal a rose. He's the thief, and quickly condemned. Wow, figure that out.

So with all these thoughts in my head, is it any wonder I have such a difficult time surving in a hypocritical system which I can't understand? All my life I was told I was an animal, unfit for decent society, yet I find I have more com-passion and concern for other people than many straight people do. So I guess I am confused. Who are the good guys, and who are the bad guys? When is right right, and when is it wrong? I laugh every time I see a statue of our symbol of justice with the blindfold over her eyes. Man, she's far from blind. She sees well enough to discriminate against the poor in court.

It sickens me to read and hear about Agnew being dealt with too severely, because "after all he did a great service to this country." Bullshit! Not only did he take bribes and kickbacks, evade income tax, he also is guilty of stealing the salaries paid to him. He was elected and paid by the people to be an honest person; he wasn't, therefore he collected his salary under false pretenses, which is stealing. And even worse, he stole something I never did: he stole the trust and loyalty of millions of people, which can't ever be repaid.

Thousands of men and women have gone to prison for far lesser crimes. A prostitute sells her own body; there's no stealing involved, yet the police are quick to put her in prison. Figure that out. And Agnew's comment regarding a slum kid, "You see one, you see them all." Few men in prison are capable of such insensitive feelings. Do you realize that some of the men killed in the Attica murders were guilty of lesser crimes than Agnew committed?

I am not saying Agnew should be imprisoned. Or other politicans like him that abuse the power of their office and cheat and steal. I'm just asking you not to be so quick to send the have-nots, the poor and unfortunate ones to prison. I mean you can't say the system operates on justice and then discriminate about who gets dealt with justice and who doesn't.

A very close friend of mine just read these last dozen pages. When I asked her opinion, she replied, "It's scary. It makes you seem like two different people." Well, it's damn sure a bit scary to me also. I look at the two different persons I seem to be, the one that likes the quiet, simple country life, and the me that has to be where the "action" is. I wonder which person am I really?

Through experience I've learned that I can't live both types of lifestyles. In my world you can't ride the middle of the fence without being dragged down to one side or the other. Sometimes I feel like a small twig in a pond of water, being blown this way and that way with each bit of breeze.

215

My goal now is to find my "spot." A place where I can completely relax, without the feeling of being threatened by each gust of wind. A place where I can shout, "This is me, world. Please l...

**From Ed Morris's
PROLOGUE:**

"The purpose of this book is not to evoke sympathy or the attitude 'poor guy, never had a chance.' Its purpose is to awaken the public to the desperate need for the reevaluation of treatment for the neglected child and for the criminal offender.

"My story is not unique. Thousands of people have gone through life filled with the torments I suffered and filled with the same thoughts of loneliness, desperation, confusion and a need for love and acknowledgment.

"Let us begin."

Photo by Joan Bingham

Jacket design by Donya Melanson
Printed in the United States by
Federated Printing Company, Inc.

MASON & LIPSCOMB PUBLISHERS, INC.
384 Fifth Avenue
New York, N.Y. 10018